DRINK VERMONT

DRINK VERMONT

BEER, WINE, AND SPIRITS OF THE GREEN MOUNTAIN STATE

WRITING & PHOTOGRAPHY
BY LIZA GERSHMAN

Skyhorse Publishing

Visit our website at www.skyhorsepublishing.com.

10 9 8 7 6 5 4 3 2 1

Library of Congress Cataloging-in-Publication Data is available on file.

Cover design by Jane Sheppard
Cover photos by Liza Gershman

Print ISBN: 978-1-5107-2321-4
Ebook ISBN: 978-1-5107-2325-2

Printed in China

for Alastair & Mimi
and for surviving Vermont winters

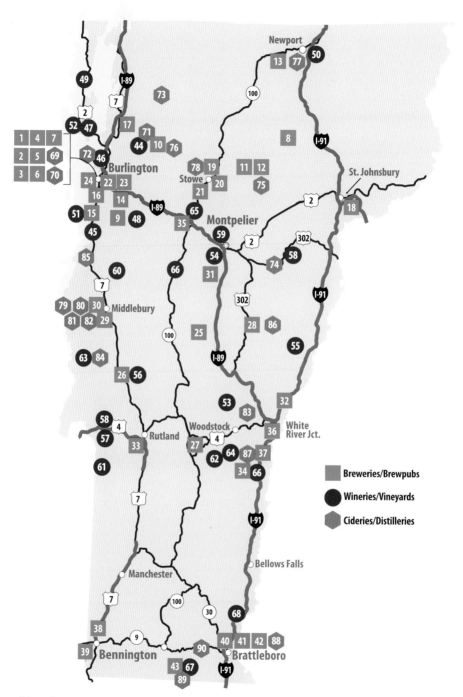

Map designed by Tim Newcomb of Newcomb Studios

Breweries and Brewpubs

Northern Vermont
1. Foam Brewers
2. Queen City Brewery
3. Simple Roots Brewing
4. Switchback Brewing Co.
5. Three Needs Taproom & Brewery
6. Vermont Pub & Brewery
7. Zero Gravity Craft Brewery
8. Hill Farmstead
9. Frost Beer Works
10. Brewster River Pub and Brewery
11. Lost Nation Brewing
12. Rock Art Brewery
13. Kingdom Brewing
14. Stone Corral Brewery
15. Fiddlehead Brewing Co.
16. Magic Hat Brewing Co.
17. 14th Star Brewing
18. Kingdom Taproom
19. The Alchemist
20. Idletyme Brewing Co.
21. von Trapp Brewery at Trapp Family Lodge
22. Burlington Beer Co.
23. Goodwater Brewery
24. Four Quarters Brewing

Central Vermont
25. Bent Hill Brewery
26. Foley Brothers Brewing
27. Long Trail Brewing Co.
28. Brocklebank Craft Brewery
29. Drop-In Brewing Co.
30. Otter Creek Brewing Co.
31. Good Measure Brewing
32. Jasper Murdock's Alehouse
33. Hop'n Moose Brewing Co.
34. Trout River Brewing Co.
35. Prohibition Pig
36. River Roost Brewery
37. Harpoon Brewery

Southern Vermont
38. Madison Brewing
39. Northshire Brewery
40. Hermit Thrush Brewery
41. McNeill's Pub and Brewery
42. Whetsone Station Brewery
43. J'ville Brewery

Wineries and Vineyards

Northern Vermont
44. Boyden Valley Winery & Spirits
45. Charlotte Village Winery
46. Hillis, Sugarbush Farm & Vineyard
47. East Shore Vineyard
48. Huntington River Vineyard at Galloping Hill Farm
49. Hall Home Place
50. Eden Ice Cider Company & Winery Inc.
51. Shelburne Vineyard
52. Snow Farm Vineyard

Central Vermont
53. La Garagista
54. Fresh Tracks Farm Vineyard & Winery
55. Three Sisters Vineyard & Winery
56. Neshobe River Winery
57. Montcalm Vineyards
58. Artesano Meadery
59. North Branch Vineyards
60. Lincoln Peak Vineyard
61. Whaleback Vineyard
62. Brook Farm Vineyards
63. Champlain Orchards
64. Brick Cape Vineyard
65. Boyden Valley Winery & Spirits Tasting Room Annex
66. Bow Vineyard & Winery

Southern Vermont
67. Honora Winery
68. Putney Mountain Winery

Cideries and Distilleries

Northern Vermont
69. Citizen Cider
70. Mad River Distillers
71. Boyden Valley Winery & Spirits
72. Groennfell Meadery, LLC
73. Elm Brook Distillery
74. Artesano Meadery
75. Caledonia Spirits Inc. Barr Hill
76. Smugglers' Notch Distillery
77. Eden Ice Cider Co.
78. Stowe Cider

Central Vermont
79. Appalachian Gap Distillery
80. Stonecutter Spirits
81. Vermont Hard Cider Company (Woodchuck Hard Cider)
82. WhistlePig Whiskey
83. Vermont Spirits
84. Champlain Orchards
85. Shacksbury Cider
86. Flag Hill Farm
87. American Crafted Spirits/SILO Distillery

Southern Vermont
88. Saxtons River Distillery
89. Honora Winery and J'ville Craft Brewery
90. Vermont Distillers

Table of Contents

Foreword

Vermont is a small state, with an outsize reputation. Our mountains, forests, lakes, and rivers make us a leader in outdoor recreation for those dreaming of escaping the stress of urban living.

Our challenging, rugged climate pulls us together in battle against the elements, and our short growing season requires creative hard work to survive. Vermont's unique personality has attracted a host of dynamic individuals to move here over the years; I often joke that many of my favorite Vermonters weren't born here, and they exemplify the passion of the *recently converted*, as they embrace the lifestyle they chose in their new home state. My family had already seen much of America when they decided to buy a farm in Vermont. It reminded them of Austria—not just the landscape, but also the hardworking, self-reliant, independent nature of the people here.

Today, this confluence of physical beauty, creativity, hard work, and the inspiration of nature has made Vermont a leader in artisan products. Long known for our maple syrup, apples, and cheeses, Vermonters have learned to add value to the natural resources available here; it was only natural to become a leader in hard cider, as well. Some of the earliest major craft breweries in the nation started in Vermont, and today we boast the most breweries per capita of any state in the United States A natural offshoot of this knowledge of fermentation science led to the creation of high-quality distilleries and wineries. My mom's favorite vodka is made in Vermont.

It's always seemed like it was my family's destiny to make our home, and our future, in Vermont. Liza will show you why so many other dynamic individuals feel the same way. Prost!

—Sam von Trapp, von Trapp Brewing

Introduction

Famed for local resources like maple and dairy, stone and wood, and the stunning colors of fall foliage, Vermont brims with a seasonal abundance like very few regions in the greater United States. *Drink Vermont* is an exploration of the flavors, people, and locations throughout the environs. You'll find interviews, recipes, and anecdotes from many of the most prominent distilleries, well-regarded breweries, cideries, and wineries. And let's not forget about the natural character and splendor that comprise the great landscape of Vermont.

Farming towns line the highways, and visitors come from the far reaches of the world to wonder at the sights, scents, and flavors that make up this New England gem.

Many Vermont products are made by craftspeople who take great pride in their work, as well as in their lineage and heritage. Cold winters and hot summers make for hearty stock, and Vermont has some of the proudest citizens in America. From coffee roasters and sugar makers to builders, dairy farmers, painters, and potters, the focus of these artisans in creating high-quality specialty goods is one of many reasons why Vermont products are in such high demand worldwide.

This book will take readers on a journey through Vermont's seasons as they discover flavors, drink recipes, travel suggestions, and more. Everything from the acclaimed Heady Topper (often voted the "Top Beer in America") to the small-town, farm-to-table cider producers, the flavors of the Green Mountain State will be celebrated and revealed.

Sustainable farming is important, especially in Vermont. Many farmers, like those at Fresh Tracks Farm, believe that the use of the land directly equates to its bounty and flavor. That is why they, like others, use renewable energy sources like solar and geothermal to heat, cool, and power their facilities. Natural farming principles are a key aspect of production for many, and working the land with a respect for both science and tradition in order to create and maintain healthy growth is essential. Sustainability for many Vermont companies is the amalgamation of business and environment, and maintaining a sense of pride in each of their choices as they move forward is vital to who they are. Vermonters in general aim to create positive work environments for employees, exceptional craftsmanship, the best products possible, and give back to their communities like few other states.

Vermont is famous for its dairy farms and apple orchards. Boyden Valley Winery & Spirits, the first craft distilled company in the United States to specialize in cream liqueurs, is an example of the fine attention to the commingling of environment and business that one hopes to see. Vermont apple brandy, cream, maple syrup, and other products are uniquely Vermont, and they make this region home to innovation in flavor in a way that is rare to see in current times.

Eden Ice Cider Company & Winery, for example, forged a path into the harsh climate offered by New England when they developed products to reflect the cold winter of Vermont and the apple heritage of the Green Mountain State. Their ciders are made with forward-thinking, while maintaining a sense of reverence for the fine, rare, and expensive local products that they source and use.

Local produce is such a crucial aspect of flavor for these brands, and many producers acknowledge the essential role that fresh fruit and quality offer to a successful beverage. These purveyors take a holistic approach to their ciders, and many offer items like apple doughnuts, spreads, and dried products.

Beer has been a staple of New England since the time of the Declaration of Independence, and Norwich Inn celebrates that proud heritage in their production. According to the inn's website, President James Monroe dined at the Norwich Inn in 1817, during a horseback tour of New England. Whether or not he had a beer is not recorded, but the inn posits that if he did, "it was most likely brewed at the inn," since Vermont had no commercial breweries at the time. Local beers were brewed in small batches, usually only enough for the brewer and his friends. Whether or not this fable is true, the long and thoughtful heritage of Vermont beer making is certainly true.

Idletyme Brewing Company, like many others, serves food, and for those who do not consider the beverages of Vermont to be food: it's a very French way of thinking, and perhaps that comes from the Québécois influence in the region.

As for local employment, the wineries, breweries, cideries, and distilleries of Vermont are certainly playing their part. The craft beer industry in the state supports over 1,500 jobs and draws in more than one million tourists every year, according to a recently commissioned Economic Impact Report. The Brewery Association currently has forty-nine members and is growing rapidly. Many of Vermont's beers have earned high praise and garnered awards like "Best in the World," year after year.

As for the wine industry, Vermont's harsh winters require a hardy vine to make it through temperatures that can plunge into the -20°F range, and colder. Most commonly known varietals that thrive in a Mediterranean climate, or in other popular wine regions like Australia, Chili, and South Africa, cannot survive in the winter climate of Vermont.

How does one produce wine in such an unforgiving climate? Like any agricultural activity, much of the success depends upon preparation and field work, which can be controlled, and weather, which is unpredictable. Snow, sleet, and hail storms can devastate vines, and Vermont has its share of them. Additionally, the high humidity of summer months can increase potential for rot on the vines. New England isn't the most ideal climate for grape growing, but producers persevere through below freezing winters and often oppressively hot summers, and that is their way of life. Despite skepticism, grape growing and wine making have been making steady inroads in Vermont, with numerous vineyards and wineries located throughout the state, and more coming. Many of these wineries have a loyal following and have shown that they too can produce award-winning products.

While the new grapes being cultivated and tested by the University of Vermont show resistance to common diseases and pests, serious vineyard issues relating to typically cold and unpredictable New England weather remain, and wineries like Mad River fight this every season. Grapes are fickle in the best of scenarios, and owning a winery in Vermont is perhaps the best metaphor for the way true Vermonters think; they can do anything, survive anything.

Marquette is an extremely strong stock, again a metaphor for Vermonters, and can survive and thrive in the below-freezing temperatures. Many wineries are experimenting with this varietal with much success. Some would argue a case against this, but like Vermonters, the grapes will prove them wrong.

Grape growers in climates like that of New England and the Upper Midwest used to be limited to a few varieties like Concord, which is commonly used in nonalcoholic juice. Although Concord grapes don't always ripen in the relatively short growing season, "even when they did ripen, they were suitable mostly for jelly and juice. But all that has changed. These cold-hardy grape varietals are being planted throughout the Northeast, Midwest, and southern Canada," says Lincoln Peak Vineyards' website. "Excellent wine is being produced and sold at these vineyards, and more vineyards are being planted as fast as the vines can be propagated. The world of grape growing has truly moved north!"

Putting in the Seed

You come to fetch me from my work to-night
When supper's on the table, and we'll see
If I can leave off burying the white
Soft petals fallen from the apple tree.
(Soft petals, yes, but not so barren quite,
Mingled with these, smooth bean and wrinkled pea;)
And go along with you ere you lose sight
Of what you came for and become like me,
Slave to a springtime passion for the earth.
How Love burns through the Putting in the Seed
On through the watching for that early birth
When, just as the soil tarnishes with weed,
The sturdy seedling with arched body comes
Shouldering its way and shedding the earth crumbs.

—Robert Frost

WINERIES

Maple syrup? Of course. Cheddar cheese? Sure. But wine grapes? It's not a crop that's long been associated with farming in Vermont. But thanks to the development of new grape varieties that thrive here, intrepid growers are planting vineyards and producing some excellent wines. Are Vermont vineyards going to compete with Napa Valley? Of course not, and that's the point.

The best Vermont wines are unique creations with wonderful flavors found nowhere else. There is plenty of variety in these wines, but to generalize, Vermont wines tend to be bright, fresh, and crisp. Sure, there are sweet wines being made—often complex and nuanced sweet wines. And there are lovely dry wines produced in Vermont as well, dry wines that often surprise and confound wine aficionados who taste them for the first time. Adventurous wine lovers who seek out the delight of unusual new wines are realizing that Vermont is a perfect place to find unexpected treasures.

For those not familiar with the varietals of the Northeast, here is a brief description:

Red Grapes

Marquette sets a new standard of excellence for winter-hardy red wine grapes. The grape is a grandchild, so to speak, of Pinot Noir but tends to have more body. The wine is complex, with characteristic black cherry and black pepper notes and more tannin than the other northern reds. The grapes mature about two weeks before Frontenac.

Frontenac is a very cold-hardy vine and has borne a full crop after temperatures as low as −30°F. Frontenac's small black berries are produced on large clusters that are usually slightly loose. It is a consistently heavy producer and sometimes requires cluster thinning. Frontenac wine has a pleasant cherry aroma with notes of plum and a garnet red color.

Petite Pearl is a newer variety from grape breeder Tom Plocher of Minnesota. With small, dense clusters and beautiful color, we're still experimenting with the potential of this grape. Our 2016 rosé has been a big hit.

White Grapes

La Crescent has long, slightly loose clusters and turns a beautiful golden-brown color when ripe. La Crescent produces a wine with a pronounced and delicious apricot flavor. The wine is fairly high in acid and would be made in a Germanic style, with some residual sugar. The wine can be very good, balanced, and with good body.

Louise Swenson is one of Elmer's grapes, named for his wife. The wine has a typically delicate aroma of flowers and honey. This wine's only fault is that it is rather light in body. Blending with a variety such as Prairie Star makes it a more complete wine. Louise Swenson rarely exceeds twenty Brix, but acidity is moderate.

Prairie Star, another of Elmer's varieties, has small, light-colored berries. Prairie Star has good body, and so we blend it with others of Elmer's grapes. The vine is one of the hardiest white wine varieties, suffering little damage in all but the harshest winters.

Swenson White clusters are medium-large and rather loose. The berries are large and thick-skinned, allowing them to hang on the vine, unmolested by insects late into the fall season. Wines produced from Swenson White have a pronounced flowery nose and a long fruity finish.

Frontenac Gris (pronounced "gree") is a natural variant of Frontenac with dusky purple/gray fruit ("gris" is "gray" in French). Frontenac Gris makes a wine with a peach flavor and tropical fruit/grapefruit undertones. The wine color ranges from amber to light rosé, depending on how long the juice sits with the skins.

Frontenac Blanc is a natural variant of Frontenac Gris with light berries but some Frontenac family characteristics, like large, leggy clusters and good winter hardiness. Frontenac Blanc wine tends to be austere, and it makes great blending with some Swenson varieties.

Table Grapes

Somerset Seedless is a seedless grape with small, orange-red berries and good flavor. Many folks say it's the best table grape they've ever had. The vines are hardy to about −30°F. The fruit ripens mid- to late-August.

—Sara & Chris Granstrom, Owners, Lincoln Peak Vineyard

Artesano Meadery

Groton

Using the best natural local ingredients, Artesano Meadery produces a range of products that include tonics, vinegar, and wine made from honey. Artesano's mission is clear: know what you put into your body and know where those ingredients come from. Located in Groton, Vermont, Artesano's handcrafted mead, vinegar tonic, and ice cream are small-batch products that can be enjoyed perennially.

A key selling point in Artesano's local, all-natural products is that they only use honey for added sweetness. *www.artesanomead.com*

Boyden Valley Winery & Spirits

See under "Distilleries."

Brook Farm Vineyards

Ludlow

In 2008, Doug and Jennifer McBride became the owners of Brook Farm. Formerly a New York attorney, Doug and his wife, Jennifer (the founder and owner of a couture textile design business), moved to Vermont in search of a quieter life. When they fell in love with Brook Farm, they saw the possibility of marrying their passion for Vermont to their interest in wine.

Brook Farm Vineyards strives to create consistent wine. From the first steps in the vineyard, through the cellaring process, great care is taken to ensure quality and uniformity in flavor. The winemakers specifically focus on texture, structure, and vinifera, using Brook Farm's natural resources to make the best possible product. Fortunately for the McBrides, the farm is situated on a terroir that encompasses rocky slopes and sandy loam soil. This soil yields wines from seven different cold-hearty varietals and produce the following wines: La Crescent, Edelweiss, Frontenac Rose, Marquette, and Twenty Mile Red. *www.brookfarmvineyards.com*

Champlain Orchards

Shoreham

Family owned and operated, Champlain Orchards is one of the oldest continuously operating orchards in Vermont and has an eye toward ecology and sustainability.

More than a winery, Champlain Orchards grows upwards of 100 varieties of apples, plums, peaches, nectarines, pears, raspberries, cherries, and blueberries, all on 220 acres. Self-proclaimed stewards of the land, Champlain adheres to the strictest Eco Apple requirements while simultaneously acting to maintain a minimal carbon footprint.

Like many other wineries in Vermont, Champlain Orchards is conscious of sustainability not only in their products, but in their relationship with the community as well.

Champlain Orchards employs over thirty locals year-round, and thirty seasonal workers, delivering to the community through schools, hospitals, CSAs, restaurants, and more.

Bill Suhr, the owner, often remarks, "I was just trying to grow some apples!" when he humbly spoke about their large production. But Champlain is achieving quite a bit more than something as simple as that.

www.champlainorchards.com

CHARLOTTE VILLAGE WINERY

Charlotte

Founded in 2001 by fourth generation Vermonters, William and Colleen Pelkey and their son, Will Pelkey, the winery began producing blueberry wines with the blueberries from a 10-acre field. This passion for wine continued, and now they include grape wine in their portfolio. Today, Charlotte Village's many visitors sip their wine and look to the famed view of the Adirondacks from the winery's large deck.

Products include Strawberry Riesling Wine, Raspberry Wine, Peach Chardonnay Wine, and three styles of Blueberry Wine. Grape varietals are Merlot, Cabernet Sauvignon, Gamay, and Pinot Grigio.

www.charlottevillagewinery.com

EAST SHORE VINEYARD

South Hero

Started by childhood friends Hal Evans and Ben Durant, East Shore Vineyard is a hidden treasure located within Vermont's Champlain Islands. They planted their first vines on Grand Isle, which has a microclimate similar to that of Northern Europe, more than a decade ago.

Now these lifelong friends produce red, white, and sparkling wines at their Landon Farm in South Hero, which is easily accessed by car from Vermont or by ferry from New York state.

www.eastshorevineyard.com

EDEN ICE CIDER COMPANY & WINERY

See under "Ciders."

Fresh Tracks Farm Vineyard & Winery

Berlin

Located in Central Vermont, Fresh Tracks Farm, founded in 2002, is proud to produce wine in such a demanding climate. After years of hard work and dedication preparing the property for its first vintage, Christina Castegren, winemaker and proprietor, and a team of colleagues and friends now produce six strong varietals.

"Eventually, we planted three grapes for jam production and one edible variety for our afternoon snacks. In 2006, we produced our first vintages of Little Piggy Pink, Vermont Rosé, and Frontenac Gris," Castegren remarked. "During this period, we ventured into maple syrup, grape jam, and red wine vinegar production as well, and it all took place in our little red barn up on the hill."

Wine making for Castegren began with her passion for chemistry, and a love for farming and the outdoors. "But not just any farming," she continued. "Annuals die each year, and I wanted a relationship with plants as well as the land. Growing grapes fit all of that, except for the weather. My neighbors experienced a lot of head turning and scratching."

The winery's flagship product is the Marquette; there's some Pinot in its parentage. The grape expresses well in the cold Vermont environment and makes for an interesting product.

"The maple wine is really extraordinary and different," remarked Castegren. "We have 1,100 maple taps. We use only our own fruit. And we put a lot of effort into our packaging. For example, we have a local artist create the labels."

Sustainable farming is at the heart of everything they do at Fresh Tracks Farm Vineyard & Winery. As their website states, "Sustainable farming is important, especially in Vermont. We believe that how we live on the land has a direct impact on what we receive from it. That's why we use renewable sources like geothermal and solar energy to heat, cool, and power our wine facility. We also draw on a variety of natural farming principles and work the land with a respect for both science and tradition to foster healthy growth. For us, sustainability is also about running a business that we can feel proud of. We strive to provide value to our community, a high-quality product to our customers, and a positive working environment for everyone here at Fresh Tracks Farm." For example, they have a weeding machine rather than using weed sprays. "This is a farming community and we're proud to be a part of that," Castegren said.

As for barrels, the winery started with American oak and French oak, but over time they began switching to Hungarian oak.

The upper vineyard covers twelve acres and contains Marquette, St. Croix, Frontenac, Frontenac Gris, La Crescent, and Adalmiina grapes, along with Mars and Bluebell. Frontenac, Beta, and "King of the North" are grown on a site behind the winery.

"Our approach to winemaking at Fresh Tracks Farm is dynamic and both reflects and respects the many nuances of each unique vintage," Castegren said. "Originally, our winery was housed in a red barn, up on the hill. The wine was made in a few stainless steel tanks, using a small basket press. Now, in our new production facility, we have a range of modern equipment and a robust lab with which to closely monitor the production of our wines. Visible from the tasting bar, we have approximately fourty oak barrels of varying origin housed in a temperature-regulated 'cave.'"

Another interesting fact about Fresh Tracks Farm is that they are female owned and operated, which is rare in this male-dominated industry. "There are not a lot of women winemakers," said Castegren. "I'm the owner and winemaker, and the other winemaker also happens to be a woman."

www.freshtracksfarm.com

Hall Home Place Ice Cider

Isle La Motte

Located in the scenic Hall's Orchard of Isle La Motte, the acreage has belonged to the Halls for many generations, dating back to the late-1700s. With a strong heritage of apple and pear cultivation, this newest generation of Halls uses the cryoconcentration approach to cider making, which means that the apples are harvested in January after the frosts and cold freeze.

The sweet cider, largely controlled by the elements of the outdoor temperature, is pressed in late December.

Once the two apple groupings are harvested, they are then often combined and ground and pressed.

The double pressing allows for the sweet cider to already have a distinct flavor before it is blended with the remaining fruit. The sweet cider is then stored outside until it freezes into a solid state and the high sugar concentrate melts off, revealing a product that is then collected for ice cider processing after the fact. Once this juice is ready to go through the fermentation process, Hall uses a process that is standard to most wine production; however, the high sugar levels dictate a different "feeding of yeast" that one sees in typical wine making.

The sweet cider concentrate that they use is always above thirty-two Brix. As they explain on the website, "We stop the fermentation process by putting the ice cider back outside to kill any remaining yeast. As another aside, March 2012 was way too warm to easily do this. We age our ice cider for different periods of time. We are always searching for the right taste and have found some blends are best when aged for a long time while others are ready sooner."

The fruit used by Hall is processed in hydraulic water bladder presses, which gives them great flexibility in the pressing process because the size allows for larger volume than other presses. "We can press as little as fifteen to eighteen gallons at a time," states the website. "However, depending on the amount of cider produced daily, between 40 and 900 gallons of water can flow through them. We have built a closed loop water system in which water is pumped from a separate holding tank to the presses. Then when the press is complete, instead of the water going out as waste, it is pumped back in the holding tank. An added benefit to this is that the pumping out of the press allows for a faster press cycle."

Fact: it takes about one bushel of apples to make two-and-a-half to three gallons of sweet cider, and they make a lot of sweet cider.

Once the apples are pressed, the skins and cores remain, leaving a "pumice" substance. Wasting nothing, the spent pumice is then returned to the orchard and becomes sustenance for the wild deer and the property's pigs.

As for their ice cider, the guidelines, developed in Quebec, Canada, in the early-1990s, are much like the practices of making ice wine, in that apples for cider, like grapes for ice wine are required to stay on the tree through a hard frost or a freeze. Cryoconcentration, one of the two commonly used practices for making ice cider, dictates a late harvest and is followed by a fresh storage process through December. At this stage in production, the apples can then be pressed and the juice can freeze through its own natural cycle. A month later, what is known as "cold fermentation" begins.

The second process, known as cryoextraction, is a more traditional system and requires the fruit to remain on the trees through January. When the weather drops to between 5°F and 18°F consistently, the fruit is harvested and stored to cold ferment for a number of months (this time frame varies, depending on the desired schedule of the producer). www.hallhomeplace.com

HILLIS' SUGARBUSH FARM & VINEYARD

Colchester

Hillis' Sugarbush Farm & Vineyard was established in 1987, producing wool, meat, poultry, and maple syrup. The vineyard was added in 2007, with the first wines offered for sale in 2010. The farm is comprised of seventy-seven acres in two locations, the original Colchester parcel on Sugarbush Farm Road and Butler Island Vineyard, which is located on Butler Island in northern Lake Champlain.

The specialty at this family-run operation is the fusion of wine and maple, as can be tasted in their Red Maple, Sugarbush Nectar, Candy Apple, and the vineyard's 100 percent maple wine, Maple Ambrosia. www.hillisfarm.com

HUNTINGTON RIVER VINEYARD

Huntington

Located on the sloping hills at Galloping Hill Farm, Huntington River Vineyard grows nine varieties of grapes, all of which are cold-hardy. This is essential for successful vineyard management in New England. The grapes are used to produce six different wines:

Marquette, cousin of Frontenac and grandson of Pinot Noir, with distinct notes of blackberry, cherry, and black current flavors.

Frontenac has flavors of cherry, berry, and plum.

Frontenac Gris exhibits tropical flavors and a touch of honey.

La Crescent is the flagship white wine and offers fruit flavors and fragrant floral aromas.

Giddy Up has flavors of pear and light floral notes.

Star Grazing offers notes of fruit and honey with a floral character. www.huntingtonrivervineyard.com

Lincoln Peak Vineyard

Middlebury

"It all started back in 2001 with a shoebox full of grapevine cuttings from a fellow in Minnesota," said owner Chris Granstrom. "I had heard about these new, winter-hardy grape varieties, and I sent him an email. I stuck the cuttings in the ground; they grew. Within a few years, grapes took over our strawberry fields, and now we find ourselves one of the largest grape producers in the state of Vermont."

Many of Lincoln Peak's wines came from a successful enological breeding program at the University of Minnesota. "It's an old-fashioned process," said Granstrom about "moving pollen from one flower to another, planting the resulting seed, evaluating the plants and the grapes, and then starting again."

He explained, "Grape growers in places like New England and the Upper Midwest used to be limited to a few varieties like Concord. Even these grapes didn't always ripen in our relatively short growing season, and even when they did ripen, they were suitable mostly for jelly and juice."

Today the narrative is very different, as cold-hardy varietals are taking center stage in the wine industry and producers in the Northeast are garnering attention from critics and connoisseurs alike.

"Some folks may have thought we were crazy to start an enterprise like this," said Granstrom. "But with some good land, careful farming techniques, a great farm crew, and support from our neighbors, it's all working out. We like to think that we're helping to turn a new page in Vermont's long and varied agricultural history."

Granstrom and his wife, Sara, began farming their land in 1981, when Chris started an apple tree nursery. He grafted and sold trees for ten years, while the couple established a successful strawberry farm on the property. "The strawberry enterprise took off; folks used to line their cars up in the morning waiting for us to open our gates," remembered Chris. "The strawberries were good to us for more than twenty years, but the promise of the new, cold-hardy grape varieties caught our attention, and we started off on a new enterprise yet again."

The then-small greenhouse was used to propagate grapevines, which the Granstroms then sold to other Vermont upstart vineyards for a number of seasons before their entire strawberry crop became grapevines. "The grapes thrived here, and the wine was good. A new chapter in the life of this farm—and family—had begun," remarked Chris.
www.lincolnpeakvineyard.com

Mad River Vineyard

Waitsfield

Started by four friends—Joe and Carol Klimek, Tom Golodik, and Kathleen Rubel—Mad River Vineyard was an amalgamation of friendship and a deep passion for Vermont.

In June 2007, the first vines were planted, but this was not an overnight venture. The four friends spent years cultivating their land, studying vineyards in Napa and Europe, and learning all they could about grape varietals, equipment, terroir, and weather.

Climatic considerations, as others have mentioned, are the principal concern for any winemaker in Vermont. Not only do you need hardy root stock and a familiarity of best practices from around the globe, but one must have tremendous patience as well.

In wine, much of the flavor comes from terroir, and any talented viticulturist will tell you that soil preparation is of the utmost concern. Weather is of course the next success factor, and grapes need the measured recipe of "sun, rain when needed—but not too much, low humidity, no hail storms that can devastate the vines," they explain on the website.

Like all other Vermont wine producers, Mad River Vineyard is at the whim of Mother Nature, and a number of spring frosts have left a great deficit in the vineyard's offerings.

Outside of weather concerns, Vermont winemakers must face the same pest interference that winemakers around the world fear. Varietals commonly used in Vermont are newer grapes, often developed in university labs, which can offer some excellent resistance to many of the most common rots and pests.

In addition, Mad River Vineyard has found a unique control method for Japanese beetles, as explained on the website: "Japanese beetles love to visit us in late spring and early summer, ripping through the vineyard and reducing leaves to lacy ghosts of their former selves. The beetles are large and easily seen. Joe's approach has been to offer his grandchildren a penny bounty for each they bring in—it's amazing how fast young ones learn how to count to large numbers and deal with financial transactions while cleaning out the vineyard!"

Mad River Vineyard focuses on vineyard management and grows grapes for many wine producers in Vermont. Grape varietals include Marquette, Petite Pearl, and Frontenac. *www.madrivervineyard.com*

While you're in Vermont's Mad River Valley, stop in at the Madsonian Museum of Industrial Design, where they have everything from cars to toasters and toys to canoes. The collection showcases work by designers such as Frank Lloyd Wright, Ludwig Mies, Norman Bel Geddes, and Marcel Breuer.

Montcalm Vineyards

Castleton

Owned by Ray Knutsen, Montcalm Vineyards, like many others, was heavily influenced by the University of Minnesota viticulture program. But where it all started for Knutsen, in the summer of 1978, was on a walk on his family's Vermont farm with his college roommate. According to their website, Knutsen's roommate "was a horticulture major and a complete 'wine geek.' When he saw our gray slate soils, southern exposure, and enormous wild grape vines, he said it was an ideal vineyard site. He said, 'This is what they grow Riesling on in Germany! You have to plant a vineyard!'" The following summer, Knutsen planted his first small experimental vineyard with the help of the vinicultural department from Cornell, where he obtained his first root stock. "Unfortunately, our winters proved too harsh for the tender European vines, and they died," said Knutsen, who wasn't defeated and continued his experimentation with planting.

In 1999, Knusten had a conversation with an elderly German nursery owner from the Finger Lakes in New York state that changed the course of his future forever. "I heard he had a clone of Riesling that might be slightly more winter-hardy than the commonly planted cultivars. He said he had it, and he would send me some, but assured me they would fail in Vermont. He was right. However, in that same conversation he told me about a new variety that was recently released by the University of Minnesota that was winter-hardy to about about -30°F. He sent me my first twenty-five vines, and they not only survived but thrived on my vineyard site. Finally, after twenty years of disappointment, there was a glimmer of hope."
www.montcalmvineyards.com

Neshobe River Winery

Brandon

Robert and Ronda Foley founded the Neshobe River Winery with an eye toward small production and sustainability. The project is entirely run by the family, with Patrick Foley as the winemaker, Christine Foley as head of hospitality, and Dan Foley as the vineyard manager. The facility is located in the foothills of the Green Mountains, is bordered by the fifth hole of the Neshobe Golf Club in the back, and the Neshobe River runs through the front of the property. The winery offers a variety of products for visitors to enjoy. Other points of interest in Brandon include hiking and biking trails, birding, and the beautiful 400,000-acre Green Mountain National Forest. With an abundance of local sites, animals, and agriculture, Brandon prides itself on being artsy, charming, and historic.
www.neshoberiverwinery.com

Newhall Farm

Reading

A prolific apple producer, Newhall Farm has more than 400 acres of estate-certified organic apple orchards and vineyard that yield their signature ice cider and apple brandy. Dedicated to sustainable farming, Newhall's farming practice includes a successful and thoughtful animal husbandry program, and a responsibility toward land conservation. The farm produces additional Vermont heritage products, including maple syrup, honey, grass-fed beef, and pastured lamb. No growth hormones or fed antibiotics are ever used. Current production includes wine from Marquette, Frontenac, Petite Pearl, La Crescent, and Frontenac Gris grapes, and the Farm is going to make brandy soon.

With the new industry of ice cider, Newhall's plentiful apple crops had a new outlet. "Little did we know, Newhall Farm would soon have a plethora of apples into which *something* must be made," states the website. "Ice cider was first on our minds. With America's rejuvenation of hard cider, Vermont is re-embracing the apple. The Pilgrims planted the first US apple trees, and today we see a metamorphosis in the apple neighborhoods of this now again fruit of choice. Pomology, the science of apple growing, is alive and well, as gnarly old apple orchards awake to a pruning saw!"

Newhall currently uses a slow drip method, rather than a vacuum pump, to extract a high-sugar concentrated sap from the trees. This process is natural, allowing for gravity to take control and let the free-run flow produce a maple syrup that, as described on the website, "has a taste of place of the Alps at Newhall Farm."
www.newhallfarmvt.com

North Branch Vineyards

Montpelier

Family owned and operated since 2007, North Branch Vineyards is located beside the North Branch River in the state's capital city, Montpelier. Here they produce a unique selection of wines by focusing on grapes grown in the region. The selection includes Simply Grace, a semi-sweet white wine with a hint of kiwi made with a blend of Seyval Blanc and Cayuga grapes. Award-winning wines include the vineyard's Frontenac Gris; Miss Maeve, with a rich raspberry ending; Traminette; Lacrescent, which features an intense apricot nose; Marquette; Saint Croix, with hints of cherry and vanilla; and Vidal Blanc ice wine, made with grapes left on the vine and harvested after temperatures drop below 15°F, which increases the sugar content.
www.northbranchvineyards.com

PUTNEY MOUNTAIN WINERY

Putney

Founded in the basement of their home in the 1990s, Putney Mountain's owners, Kate and Charles Dodge, have expanded into town and now produce a dozen wines and several sparkling juices.

Putney Mountain focuses on making non-sweet fruit wines; there are no grape-sourced wines here to speak of, and everything is aged in stainless steel.

When they first began producing wine, Charles was a professor of music at Dartmouth College and "became intrigued by his graduate students' stories of brewing beers for fun," he said. Although he contemplated brewing beer, Dodge realized that the couple had a deep interest in wine that was enhanced by their travels around the world.

The Cassis, the most award-winning beverage on their list, is what they consider to be their "flagship beverage." Charles's personal favorite really depends on the time of year. He said, "I really like our Simply Ginger Liqueur. I'm also enjoying our pear wine . . . and the blueberry."

What's going to be new in 2017 and 2018? This year will be the first time Putney Mountain distributes products out of state, which is a large step toward recognition and greater expansion for them. "We're also releasing three liqueurs: Simply Ginger, an apple brandy with a little added maple syrup, and another one I can't talk about currently," said Dodge. Whatever the secret new product is, it is sure to be well loved by their loyal followers in Vermont.

"We have been making Apple Pommeau for a while now. It's a blend of sweet cider and apple brandy. It's aged, but not in barrels," explained Dodge. "Our customers really appreciate what we are doing and say that we make the best fruit wines out there. And that we make it from good fruit, not juices. Our goal is to bring out the character of the fruit. Not just to make them 'easy drinking.'"

Putney Mountain continues to receive awards as their product line grows, and the winery attributes that to not only fantastic quality products, but the dedication that they have toward maintaining status as a Vermont Certified Green Business. *www.putneywine.com*

Shelburne Vineyard

Shelburne

Ken Albert began his career working as an engineer at IBM. This position took him to Quebec on constant business trips, and Albert developed a curiosity and passion for wine. Albert's land was leased from Shelburne farms, and he started a viticultural project. Albert partnered with friend and neighbor, Scott Prom (also an engineer), and utilizing their at-home winemaking experience and a number of courses on oenology at Cornell they released their first commercial vintage in 2000.

They decided to purchase the land, and the winery, in keeping with the sustainable efforts of many in Vermont, is LEED-designed and is surrounded by their flagship Marquette vines.

Ethan Joseph, head winemaker and vineyard manager, went to the University of Vermont for the Natural Resources program. "A friend had done some work at the vineyard, and I started working there sporadically," he noted. "I was a homebrewer for beer and cider by the time I graduated UVM, working on a grant. Then Shelburne completed their new wine facility and was looking for a full-timer with ties into sustainability."

The newest venture for the vineyard is a process called "orange wine," which takes a white grape and treats it like a red grape. Joseph explained, "In other words, rather than pressing the juice from white wine grapes and fermenting it, the grapes are fermented on the skins for a while to intensify the color and tannins. We made an orange wine with La Crescent . . . [it] sat on the skins for fifty days. Currently in a few barrels, sur lie." Sur lie is the aging process in which the finished wine sits on the lees to extract flavors. "The acidity is still crisp even though it's gone through malolactic fermentation. We're using bâtonnage on all the reds; it's nice for rounding out a mid-palate mouthfeel," said Joseph.

Joseph said, "The key to what we are doing is managing these hybrid grapes. We meticulously manage the canopy, much like it is done in California. It takes time, but the wines are better for the extra effort."

The flagship beverage is The Shelburne Vineyard Marquette, which is made from 100 percent Marquette stock from Vermont. The Shelburne Vineyard Marquette spent six months in American and French oak barrels, and there's a limited supply, since only 842 cases were produced. The vineyard's 2013 vintage produced a dry, medium-bodied red wine with notes of black cherries, spice, soft tannins, and a complex, lingering finish.

"Today's wine comes from what may seem like an unlikely place," said Joseph. "In fact, we've been on a binge of sorts recently trying wine from all kinds of unusual places to find the best to bring to you. Places like Macedonia, Moldova,

Morocco, India, Texas, Turkey, and even Vermont," he continued. "Yes, Vermont. While Vermont lies at approximately the same latitude as places like Bordeaux and the Willamette Valley, it's not usually a place you would think of for good wine thanks to its cold winters and short summers. Modern science, however, has stepped in, and with the development of hybrid grapes that can survive and even thrive in these conditions, a whole new world has opened for cool-climate regions."

What's going to be new in 2017 and 2018? "In addition to our orange wine we will be releasing a Pét-Nat. We'll be using a wild fermentation for this," Joseph said.

Shelburne ages most of its red wine in barrels, with some in American oak and a little in French oak. "But we're finding that the Hungarian oak really works well with the Marquette," said Albert.

Shelburne Vineyard is serious about sustainability. "When we bottle the wines, we use lighter weight glass bottles. We grow grass between the vines to help prevent erosion. We use gravel instead of asphalt to help prevent runoff. We work with local nonprofits. Including refugee resettlement—we have some refugees help us during harvest."

They stay busy at the vineyard hosting various events and activities including concerts, storytelling, weddings, private events, paint and sip parties, and color between the vines.

"We have a new line of wine created with spontaneous, native fermentation. The line will be called Iapetus: this is the name of the ancient ocean that covered the Lake Champlain region."

www.shelburnevineyard.com

Snow Farm Vineyard

South Hero

Located on an island in the middle of beautiful Lake Champlain, Snow Farm Winery, founded in 1992, aims to preserve Vermont's agricultural land "in the face of rapid development by providing an alternative for farmers," the owners state on the website. "With land becoming more valuable for its development potential than for its worth farming, we were concerned with the future of our state, afraid of losing what makes Vermont unique. It is our hope that we can provide an alternative for farmers, so that they can rededicate their land to a new agricultural pursuit and keep it working rather than selling it for residential or commercial purposes. Supporting us supports our mission of keeping the land open and working."

Snow Farm grows more than thirty varieties of grapes in quantities ranging from twenty-seven rows to a few plants. Varieties include Pinot Noir and Riesling, as well as the cold-hardy French hybrids, Vidal Blanc and Baco Noir. They also offer an ice wine that is well liked.

Wines offered by Snow Farm include Estate Seyval Blanc, Estate Vidal Blanc, American Riesling, Snow White, Estate Leon Millot, Estate Baco Noir, Estate Marquette, Crescent Bay Red, and Rose Red. Also available is the 2012 Estate Vidal Blanc Ice Wine with hints of mango, pineapple, and lychee nuts.

The unique microclimate of the Champlain Islands is ideal for growing cold-hardy grapes. Although their growing season is identical to that of Napa or Burgundy, France, the vinifera grapes are what survive. Harvest is typically in September, and ripe grape clusters are transported back to the winery to go through de-stemming, pressing, and crushing. The wine is fermented in stainless steel or oak and then hand-bottled and labeled at the winery.

Snow Farm celebrates harvest with live music and food in the vines. Their famed grape stomp competition, wagon rides, story walk through the vines, face painting, and crafts are not to be missed.

The January 2009 *Wine Spectator* (Editor's Choice Edition) mentioned Snow Farm as one of only five wineries whose wines have come to their attention from the forty-six smaller wine-producing states in America. This achievement for Snow Farm is an achievement for Vermont as well, putting the little-known region on the greater wine map for the world to see.

www.snowfarm.com

Whaleback Vineyard

Poultney

Whaleback Vineyard, located on an old farm in Poultney, Vermont, produces rosés, red wines, and the local favorite: apple wine. Whaleback Vineyard's nine acres yield more than 6,000 vines.

Varietals include St. Croix, Marquette, Frontenac, and Ruby Red, a sweet red blend. Their white wines are Frontenac Gris, La Crescent, Frontenac Gris Rosé, an apple wine, two dessert wines (peach and pear), and an apple ice cider.

Whaleback's tasting room is a true draw for visitors and is located inside a colonial farmhouse overlooking the vineyard. Here, spectators can view the entire winemaking process, from vine to bottle.

The great challenge that they face as a Vermont winery, like others, is the colder climate. And like those of many other producers, the vines that they have are derived from rootstock that was developed at the University of Minnesota. As they explain on the vineyard website, "combined with other cold weather techniques, these grapes have allowed us to bring local wine to our part of Southern Vermont." *www.whalebackvineyard.com*

Summer Silence

Eruptive lightnings flutter to and fro
Above the heights of immemorial hills,
Thirst-stricken air, dumb-throated, in its woe
Limply down-sagging, it's limp body spills
Upon the earth. A panting silence filsl
The empty vault of Night with shimmering bars
Of sullens silver, where the lake distils
Its misered bounty. —Hark! No whisper mars
The utter silence of the untranslated stars.

—e. e. cummings

DISTILLERIES

WHY VERMONT DISTILLERIES MATTER

Vermont is a state of incredible natural landscapes, and our farms, sugar bushes, ski mountains, lakes, rivers, and fertile valleys produce not only a huge variety of agricultural products, but also an array of one-of-a-kind experiences. We are rich in resources both land-based and people-based, and our wealth is in the dizzying array of ways we utilize those resources. We are a state committed to preservation and protection, yet we are most engaged when we share our bounty with visitors at our numerous resorts, state parks, farmers' markets, and festivals. The distillers in Vermont have each carved out a distinct way to utilize our wealth of ingredients to produce spirits that speak to this agricultural diversity.

Whether designing a still with repurposed parts and good ol' Yankee ingenuity, powering a bottling line with solar energy, or fermenting locally grown ingredients, the distillers of Vermont are resourceful, meticulous, and motivated to produce not only the best products in New England, but also some of the most memorable.

Our spirits are character-driven and reflect the influence of our picturesque mountains and valleys, and we hope you enjoy them as much as we enjoy making them. —Mimi Buttenheim, President, Mad River Distillers

APPALACHIAN GAP DISTILLERY

Middlebury

Appalachian Gap, owned by Chuck Burkins and Lars Hubbard, is an artisanal distillery in the heart of Vermont. "Few things give us as much pleasure as being able to say, 'We made this.' There is magic in the process, and magic in the glass," said Burkins.

They produce artisanal spirits by hand in a solar-powered distillery, with every one of "our spirits made right, and made right here," said Burkins. "Our spirits have layers of flavor, with distinct notes that express their ingredients, and all of them are stupidly smooth."

"We make a good pair," Burkins said of him and his co-owner. "I have a deep understanding of distillation and all the processes thereof. Lars and I are really good at figuring out what's going to taste good long before we make it."

Burkins explained, "We started as homebrewers. We remember the pride of being able to place a pint of really good beer in front of a friend (or acquaintance, or stranger); to see the widening of the eyes as they tasted how good it was; and to be able to say, 'I made that.'" In 2010, Burkins took a class on distilling one weekend in Geneva, New York, and that turned into what he calls "a mild obsession."

Ridgeline, a barrel-aged whiskey, is the distillery's flagship spirit. "This is why we started Appalachian Gap," said Burkins, whose goal is "to make beautiful, balanced, complex whiskey." The Snowfall Vermont Whiskey has been popular for more than a year, "and we have been putting a lot of it in a variety of barrels to create Ridgeline: new oak barrels, ex-bourbon barrels, and port wine barrels. We are not taking the shortcut that so many small distilleries do and trying to use smaller barrels to simulate age—we are letting it age gracefully. We won't put it into bottles until it is ready . . . and our first batches are ready," Burkins noted.

Blue Agave and Maple Syrup was created to honor the state butterfly of Vermont, which travels thousands of miles every autumn from the Green Mountains to spend the winter in Mexico, according to Burkins. The tequila has a finish with the rich, roasted, complex flavor of good maple syrup. "We can't call it tequila —only spirits distilled in certain parts of Mexico can use that name —but we think of it as . . . VTquila."

Snowfall, one of the distillery's most popular spirits, is made from corn, barley, and rye mash. "In distillation," Burkins continued, "the best part of the alcohol run is called the heart: even at full strength, it is not harsh, but sweet and almost delicate in flavor. Snowfall is the unaged heart of our Ridgeline Vermont Whiskey."

Appalachian Gap's customers describe the spirits as "all delicious and all very smooth. So, I'd say that's what sets us apart," said Burkins, who boasts that their small tasting room "is staffed by the owner and head distiller, where stories and samples are free."
www.appalachiangap.com

Boyden Valley Winery & Spirits

Cambridge

Boyden Valley Winery & Spirits is situated on a beautiful stretch of farmland west of Jeffersonville, Vermont. The property has 8,000 grapevines and 100 acres of maple trees. Founded by David and Linda Boyden, the company was the first licensed winery in Vermont, making the couple true pioneers.

From planting until the first harvest, the vines take a number of years to properly develop. While waiting for grapes to harvest, the Boydens experimented with fruit wines, like the Cranberry Wine, which has become one of their most sought-after and iconic products. Boyden's strong partnerships with other Vermont farmers were forged in these early days, and their philosophy of sustainability and stewardship have been well respected and emulated by their peers. "We compost all the grape pomace, the lees from the fermentation, grape vine clippings, manure, straw. It all goes back on the land," Boyden said.

"We started with a couple of apple wines and a hard cider. We were looking for a way to diversify the products that we could make from the farm when we started making wine," Boyden explained.

Sourcing for wine in Vermont can be an unusual task, and they began by sourcing "some French hybrids, but when the Marquette stock came out of Minnesota, we switched to that," Boyden noted.

The winery's Big Barn Red is full-bodied and a treat to sample, but Boyden's true talent comes through in the ice wines, maple crème liqueur, and hard ice cider.

The much-loved Apple Cider comes from a nearby farm. Boyden said, "We use a blend of fresh apples, not juice, from trees like Northern Spys, Empires . . . it's very artisan. We have someone else distill the apple brandy. We blend it with cream and maple syrup. We have another product that's made with ice cider. Next, we are coming out with an aged apple brandy. It will only be available at the winery to start."

Boyden Valley Winery continues to push the envelope. They are the only distillery in the nation to produce Vermont Ice Maple Cream Liqueur, their most popular product. It's a blend of their own maple syrup, Vermont Apple Brandy, Vermont Ice Cider, and cream.

What's going to be new in 2017 and 2018? "We'll be releasing a Marquette reserve," Boyden said. "It will have spent two years in the barrel and will be available only at the winery. Additionally, we're renovating the winery; we have some custom-made tanks from Italy coming in."
www.boydenvalley.com

CALEDONIA SPIRITS

Hardwick

In 2011, Todd Hardie, owner of Honey Gardens Apiaries, approached Ryan Christiansen about working on a project to distill honey wine into spirits. During the first year in business, Caledonia Spirits sold 235 cases of Barr Hill Gin and Barr Hill Vodka. In 2014, they started making their own barrels locally. In 2015, Christiansen purchased the company from Hardie, and this sale made way for Hardie to purchase the land that is now known as Thornhill Farm.

"My background is in brewing, with beer, but it was my fascination with fermentation that really captured me. The blind science of fermentation won me over. And that fascination expanded into kimchi, kraut, and kombucha making," Christiansen explained. "So I started a home brewing store, and on opening day the line was out the door, which showed me that other people had a similar fascination. The store soon became a full-time job, which I really saw as a stepping-stone to having my own microbrewery. As time went on and so many microbreweries opened and so much great beer was on the market, I stepped back to make sure my business plan was still viable. And it was during this time that I met Todd Hardie. He had just started his business, and I saw opportunities to help. I saw a brand-new variable set that I could play with, and it won me over. And,

honestly, I haven't had a day since that I haven't learned something."

Christiansen said, "Getting honey to ferment is one thing, but getting it to consistently [ferment] is tough. There are components to honey that we just don't know, and the bees aren't going to tell us. There's no greater fermentation challenge than honey."

He added, "We work with one group of beekeepers and kind of preselect honey based on how it will likely ferment, whether it will go into gin or vodka production. We try to keep things as consistent as possible, but you also need to capture the natural variation of the honey."

Christiansen continued, "I think our product will help people appreciate honey, and the importance of preventing hive collapse and keeping bees healthy. . . . We're trying to do more than sell products, we're trying to make products that are relevant to the area, helpful to the community, but also change the way we're all eating, drinking, and consuming."

Barr Hill Gin is the company's flagship product, and it makes up about 70 percent of the company's production. Christiansen said, "Barr Hill Gin is classic. But my personal favorite is Tom Cat [Gin]. I'm drawn to aged spirits. The whole category has some real complexity and an endless opportunity."

What's going to be new in 2017 and 2018? "We are looking at more single-barrel products, but

nothing is scheduled for release," Christiansen noted.

Customers share an overall sense of surprise when they taste the distillery's products. "Everyone goes into a gin-tasting experience expecting London dry. Then they are surprised by this balanced, sippable quality that helps them step back and look at the category differently," Christiansen said. "It reminds me of the time when beer brewers first started making more balanced and citrusy IPAs. It changed what drinkers thought about the IPA category. What we and other gin makers are doing is category expanding."

As for the stills, Caledonia Spirits, like other Vermont companies, made their own. "We bought our kettle, then we built a column, then we hired someone to build a condenser. Then we tried it and did some redesign and rework. When you take the still apart several times and rework it for the product you are trying to make, you learn so much. And when it's finally working perfectly, you know why it's working, it's yours."

The 300-gallon botanical extraction still is used for the gins. The 500-gallon pot is used for whiskey and doubles as a stripping still for the vodka. The 250-gallon column still is where they run all the vodka through. In late 2016, Caledonia was installing a 500-gallon traditional copper pot still in order to expand whiskey production.

In 2015, due to the shortage of barrels and the demand of Tom Cat, Caledonia Spirits set out to build their own barrels. They worked with local foresters, sawyers, and truckers to find sustainably harvested lumber to use to make the barrels.

Christiansen explained, "We fell upon this excellent cooper named Bob Hockert, but he didn't have any wood. So then we got hold of a forester, who was part of a sustainable wood harvest. They actually had some Vermont-raised white oak that was going to be cut down as a part of a forest thinning. Then we had to find a mill that would quarter-saw the wood, and trucks to move the wood, and on and on. There were six or seven people who had to be involved just to get lumber to Bob."

Christiansen added, "We were laughed at initially for making our own barrels, but it was an opportunity for us to learn more about a product we were handling every day."

As for sourcing ingredients locally, he said, "We used to make a product, a great product, which was the elderberry cordial. . . . But about the time it really started gaining ground, our elderberry farmers two hours north plowed their bushes under and switched to soybeans. Apparently, their business model for elderberries wasn't working. We were crushed." However, he noted that Hardie has planted about 200 elderberry bushes. "My goal is to use elderberries in multiple products, the cordial and some other products that we can at least get into development to look at. Elderberry is an incredible fruit to play with; [it's] nearly magical, and people need to be more aware of it," Christiansen said.

How does he enjoy what he creates? "My favorite way to use the Tom Cat Gin is to use it instead of bourbon in an old–fashioned," he said. "It's really bourbon focused; we're using new American oak, and in combination with the juniper we get this coniferous quality. It's almost like cedar or balsam, and that just comes right out in the old–fashioned. Also, we're advising people to try Barr Hill to make a simple gin and tonic or a Negroni."
www.caledoniaspirits.com

DUNC'S MILL

St. Johnsbury

Duncan Holaday has been developing his art of craft distilling for more than fifteen years. Holaday has revitalized traditional craft and inventing new techniques for micro distilling within the United States and is widely known for his custom still design and operation. Holaday has shared these techniques and innovations with many other purveyors, and his products have gained accolades at prestigious competitions throughout the world. Holaday's passion runs deep, and sharing that passion with others is a significant gift.

"In 1998," according to their website, "a downburst—Vermont's version of a tornado—laid down scores of century-old hemlocks. A neighbor called with the news, and Duncan (working at the time in Singapore) flew back to survey the damage. With all the fallen trees, along with the beautiful sugar maples left standing, an idea was born. From that, the first batch of maple spirits was distilled—from scratch and by hand."

Dunc's Mill, the oldest continuously operating distillery in Vermont, is known for its flagship product, Dunc's Maple Rum. The production process begins in the earliest days of spring. "We trudge through snowy acres in the hills around Dunc's Mill, tapping hundreds of native sugar maple trees," said Holaday. "We then slowly boil the collected sap, producing a sweet, robust syrup, and add it to our sugarcane rum. Smooth, satisfyingly sweet, rich yet balanced, Dunc's Mill Maple Rum brings Vermont's sugaring tradition from our woods to your glass. Notes of oak, honey, and stone fruit complement and add to the complexity of this unique treat."

Both of Dunc's Mill's rums are made from Fair Trade, organic sugarcane, and Vermont flavors. Dunc's Mill Elderflower Rum is created with Vermont elderflower blossoms and Austrian elder essence, which is infused into a light rum.

Even today, every batch of rum is handcrafted from start to finish by Holaday, founder and master distiller, using custom-built stripping and fractionating stills. Dunc's Mill is dedicated to creating artisanal spirits of the highest quality. All the products are organic and made entirely from scratch using only the finest ingredients.
www.duncsmill.com

FLAG HILL FARM

See under "Cideries."

Timothy Danahy and Harold Faircloth III, founders, distillers, and adventurers at Green Mountain Distillers.

GREEN MOUNTAIN DISTILLERS

Morrisville

The Shed, a popular Stowe restaurant, burned down in the mid-1990s. The owner added a brewery when the restaurant was rebuilt. Harold (Howie) Faircloth was hired as the brewer, and Timothy Danahy came along. Later, the pair decided to start a distillery.

"The first spirit we made was whiskey, and the first batch has been aging now for over thirteen years. We may put it on market this summer. We've also got some rye and corn whiskey that we are ready to bottle," noted Danahy.

What's going to be new in 2017 and 2018? "We recently purchased some additional acreage and we've been approved to put in a forty-by-sixty-foot event tent, where we can have up to twenty events a year, such as a whiskey fest, release parties, weddings," said Danahy. "We have 500 gallons of Stowe Cider that we're going to distill into apple brandy. We might bottle some unaged (silver) and age some of it. We have a tasting room, and we are in the process of building a new one."

The still here is unusual and handmade. "We took a Grundy tank and flipped it to serve as the body of our still; it's kind of a combo of a pot and column still," explained Danahy. Products are aged in used bourbon barrels.

Although Green Mountain Distillers isn't currently sourcing locally, "using organic grain is important to us," Danahy said. "We tried using regularly available grain when we first started sampling recipes, but it was GMO [genetically modified], and the distributors couldn't even tell us what country it came from. Then we found a co-op of organic grain farmers in Minnesota and made some sample batches from their grains. The flavor was incredible, much better. We said, 'I guess we're organic now!'"

www.greendistillers.com

MAD RIVER DISTILLERS

Warren

In 2011, while living in Boston, Maura Connolly was contemplating planting a vineyard on the farm in the Mad River Valley of Vermont that she and her husband, John Egan, had purchased. Her friends suggested that it would be better to produce something more native to the area. Egan, a life-long fan of Calvados, the French apple brandy, was intrigued enough to start researching apple brandy production. Brett Little, a friend who shared Egan's appreciation for Calvados, was immediately on board with the idea of starting a distillery, and production at Cold Spring Farm soon began.

In the mid-1900s, Cold Spring Farm was converted into a distillery, and Alex Hilton, a Warren native, renovated the old horse barn into a state-of-the-art craft distillery. In this grand undertaking, Hilton was asked to partner in the distillery project and became the general manager and distiller at MRD.

"We have produced over a half dozen different craft spirits since then, including Malvados, our flagship apple brandy," said Hilton.

The flagship beverage has changed over time, since the apple brandy can only be produced a couple of months out of the year. "What we make a lot more of and are known for is our rye whiskey and our maple rum," noted Hilton.

"The rye whiskey is my personal favorite," he continued. "It doesn't taste like any other rye I've had. We use three different ryes, and one of them is roasted, which gives it a unique toasted character."

What's new for 2017 and 2018? "We've been doing a collaboration series called Hopscotch. We partner with a local Vermont brewery; they brew one of their beers, and we distill it into a small batch Scotch-style malt whiskey," Hilton said. "Each release will be a representation of a different style of beer from these brewers."

The still itself, manufactured in a small town in Germany's Black Forest, looks steampunk chic but is completely computer controlled. "It's designed specifically to distill rum, fruit brandies, and whiskeys. What's great and unique about this still is that it has finesse, it allows the original flavor of the source material to come through. It's also efficient,

we can do four or five runs a day through it," explained Hilton. "We have a new still coming soon. It's also a pot still, made in the United States. It's a stripping still, a real workhorse. Basically, it will take the fermented wort and reduce the volume to concentrate the liquid into what are called 'low wines.' We can then run this unrefined product through the muller to finish it. This will enable us to produce a larger volume while maintaining the same high quality."

As for barrels, MRD uses new barrels to age the whiskey and rum, and the barrels are only used once. "We're sourcing them mostly from Kentucky and Minnesota and a few from upstate New York. We've also received a few from an up-and-coming cooperage here in Vermont [that uses] local oak," Hilton said.

All of their grains are sourced regionally from non-GMO sources, and they use Vermont ingredients when they are available. Hilton said, "The sugar in our rum is Fair Trade Certified and sustainably harvested. The water for our fermentations is drawn from a pure mountain spring on our farm."

The spent grain is sent to local farms as feed for cattle. "We pump it out to tanks, and the farmers come and load it onto trucks," he explained. "It's perfect. It's a great food source for the cattle and saves all of us money. A real symbiotic relationship."

www.madriverdistillers.com

Putney Mountain Winery

See under "Wineries."

Saxtons River Distillery

Brattleboro

After spending fifteen years as an engineer, Christian Stromberg wanted to do something different, so he started Saxtons River Distillery in 2006.

"It was a business that I saw that I could start small," he explained. "I was able to do it on my own, on my own property, and we had a family history of making cordials," Stromberg said.

Now, Saxtons River Distillery sells 30,000 bottles a year. Stromberg uses 1,000 gallons of Vermont maple syrup a year to make Sapling Maple Liqueur, Sapling Maple Bourbon, and Sapling Maple Rye. He buys it primarily from sugar makers in Windham County, Vermont. "The nice thing about being in Vermont—I had no shortage of good local products and great sugar makers to work with," he said. "Versus a cheese liqueur, I decided to go with a maple liqueur because I thought there would be broader appeal."

Stromberg said, "There's a Lithuanian cordial made with honey and spices called krupnikas that my family used to make for special occasions. The recipe became the basis for our sapling cordial, with maple syrup replacing the honey. There's also an older history in my family of my great-grandmother making moonshine during Prohibition and my great-grandfather selling it. It was a kind of unaged rye spirit. But they weren't making it for the flavor, it was purely for effect; [it was] probably still warm when they sold it."

His flagship beverage, and best seller, is the Sapling Maple Liqueur. Each bottle is made up of one-third maple syrup. "Maple liqueur is an infusion. Any liqueur is a sweetened flavored syrup. Our sweetener is maple syrup. We use dark syrup that has much more maple flavor to it," Stromberg explained. All of the spirits are cask aged to "add a woody, smooth flavor. They're good served straight, in simple cocktails, or even over ice cream. Vermont's maple and food reputation is key to sales," he added.

For Stromberg, quality comes first. "You're getting something that's special and wasn't mass produced, and I feel like we're delivering that," he said.

What's new for 2017 and 2018? "We will expand production this year in a new location. I have a large, scaled model made from LEGOs for the new facility at home. Once you start bringing in equipment, you don't want to move it again. It's my method, and it's fun. There's a small model in the tasting room. There will be a new tasting room there as well," Stromberg continued. "My background is in engineering, so while I'm looking at different manufacturers, I'll probably design our new still, too. I've been doing this for eleven years, and I've learned a lot about what works for what we are trying to do."

The still used by Saxtons River features a unique vacuum system they created. "We use a vacuum system that lowers the boiling point. This cooler distillation enables us to capture more of the fresh aromatics that are lost in a higher temperature still. If I use the same aromatics in the vacuum still as someone else using a hot still, the results are very different," Stromberg explained. "There are floral notes in juniper that just don't survive in a traditional still. During initial tests of the new product, now called Snowdrop Gin, the team was shocked at the scent of the juniper berries they were not able to smell in previous rounds of distilling. It's definitely not an off-the-shelf still; I designed it, and it works for us."

As for barrels, Stromberg said, "We buy new oak barrels from Kentucky, and when we're done with them a lot of local breweries are interested in using them to age their specialty beers. They get a long afterlife."

Local sourcing of ingredients is important to Stromberg. "We pick as much as we can of the juniper berries, and we use local rosemary. It's something we are working with local farmers on. It's a challenge," he noted. "We use real ingredients, not flavorings. There are other producers of maple liqueurs, but they use cheaper maple flavors, not real syrup. Same with coffee liqueurs. Our Perc Coffee Liqueur uses good coffee, and it's great. It tastes like coffee."

www.saxtonsriverdistillery.com

SHELBURNE ORCHARDS DISTILLERY

Shelburne

Nick Cowles, owner of Shelburne Orchards, grew up among the apple trees that now provide the foundation for Shelburne Orchards Distillery's Dead Bird apple brandy. The orchard is home to around 6,000 trees, with over thirty apple varieties, including Paula Reds, Ginger Gold, McIntosh, Cortland, Honey Crisp, Gala, Golden Delicious, Mutzu, and Northern Spy. Ninety percent of the apples are sold at the farm, and they are also used to make ginger cider, ginger jack, cider vinegar, and cider doughnuts.

The orchard uses an "ever-changing approach to apple growing" Cowles states on the website. This includes a commitment to the development of low-spray, organic practices, which was part of the criteria that earned the orchard the first annual Sustainable Agricultural Farm of the Year award in 1997. His growing methods allow him to stay in business while providing "the most ecologically friendly, safe eating and cooking apples."

Distilled from hard cider made from the orchard's apples, Shelburne Orchard Distillery sold its first batch of apple brandy in 2011 from its first distillation in 2009. Cowles and his team decided to let it age six more years for added smoothness and oak flavor.

The distillery uses American oak, French, Hungarian, and Romanian oak barrels, providing vanilla and caramel flavors to the brandy.

As Cowles states on the website: "This isn't any pansy-ass flavored neutral grain spirit. This is the real thing . . . made right here at our orchard from our own apples and pears. I like to call it the 'true spirit of Vermont agriculture!'"
www.shelburneorchards.com/distillery

The Shelburne Museum, with thirty-nine buildings located on more than fourty-five acres, is an unconventional and immersive experience. Put this at the top of your list when you're in Shelburne.

SILO DISTILLERY

Windsor

"We like to have fun while we work; the distillery plays a mix of rock, jam band, and dance music to the whiskey as it ages to get the barrels shakin' and extract flavor from the wood," said Chris Maggiolo, head distiller at Silo Distillery.

He became enthralled with distilling in college, although his major was historical archaeology. While on a trip to the Caribbean, he encountered a rum distiller making a single-barrel rum using a nineteenth-century steam-powered sugarcane press. When Maggiolo returned to the States, he couldn't find any rum of similar quality. His passion for flavor continued, and in 2011, Maggiolo got his master's degree in gastronomy. He then moved to Boston to work in craft beer, a homebrew store, and a distillery. In 2015, Maggiolo reached out to Peter at Silo about a job and was offered a position as a distiller, which has really set the direction and flavor of the production.

Silo's flagship beverages are Silo Bourbon and Silo Cucumber and Cacao Vodkas. Silo Reserve Gin, made with juniper berries and apples, is well regarded for its smooth texture and versatility; it can be served as a great sipper or as a base for cocktails, like a Manhattan. Solstice, a light spirit with notes of orange peel, is distilled from wheat beer from Harpoon Brewery.

What's new for 2017 and 2018? "We've got a single-malt whiskey coming out. The malt for it was smoked with apple wood and comes from Andrew at Peterson Quality Malt."

Silo is developing products from historic recipes. "Trying to bring back some of the tastes people used to enjoy," Maggiolo explained. "We try to source as many ingredients from Vermont as possible. All our grains come from here, the malt, the lavender for the vodka, the apples, it's all from Vermont. While we obviously can't grow cacao locally, we do get it from a local chocolate maker who buys direct from the farmers who grow it."

As for giving back to the Vermont ecosystem, the spent grain is used to feed the pigs at a local farm.

At Silo, the still is as unique as their story. "It's a 600-liter hybrid still from Germany that we call Carl. We can direct the vapor through one of two columns. The shorter column is the one we use for whiskeys and bourbon, and the taller one we use for the vodkas," Maggiolio said. "We have been using small barrels from a cooperage in Minnesota and recently switched to using slightly larger ones from Kentucky. We're also currently aging an Aisling whiskey, it's a wheat whiskey aged in tanks with charred ash staves."

www.silodistillery.com

SMUGGLERS' NOTCH DISTILLERY

Jeffersonville

Founded in 2010, Smugglers' Notch Distillery is owned by a father and son team, Ron and Jeremy Elliott. Ron, who retired from his career as a business executive, and Jeremy, who was a research chemist in the pharmaceutical industry, saw potential to work together. After assessing their strengths, they decided to open a distillery. "Our skill sets just meshed," said Ron. Marcia Elliott, Ron's wife, is the brains behind the marketing and promotions for the distillery, and their daughter, Dawn, also plays a part in keeping the business running and growing.

The Waterbury location is home to seventy-six twenty-five-gallon American oak barrels and has a clean, industrial feel. The products include 50ml mini bottles of vodka, gin, rum, bourbon, and wheat whiskey, which are all exclusively available in their tasting room and sit alongside a number of Vermont specialty items like bourbon barrel-aged maple syrup, and bourbon peach jam.

Smugglers' Notch's bourbon whiskey and rum are aged in American oak barrels. All bourbon is regulated by federal guidelines and must be aged in new, charred American white oak barrels.

Consistency is of the utmost importance to the Elliotts. Jeremy approves every batch, every barrel, every blend of whiskey to ensure that it's up to their standards. The rum, a decidedly different liquid from the white or spiced varieties a drinker might be familiar with, is aged in new barrels for three years, then spends one year in a former bourbon barrel to finish off the unique flavor profile. The distillery uses American oak barrels sourced mainly from Kentucky and Michigan.

"Our gin is made by taking our vodka—a distinctive start, as many gins are made with a neutral grain spirit base—and distilling it through a proprietary blend of herbs and spices, including juniper sourced from southern Vermont, and grains of paradise," said Ron. "Vermont crops are used when possible and available."

Smugglers' Notch falls along a famous bootleggers' run that was used in the 1800s to shift products during a trade embargo, and again in the 1920s during Prohibition.

Their Blend No. 802 is an 88-proof, true distilled gin that's handcrafted in small batches. The method includes "suspending a juniper berry infusion, among other botanicals, in a gin still vapor path," Ron explained. Blend No. 802 was developed over seventy-five different iterations and was ultimately decided upon after two hundred Vermonters from around the state participated in a taste-test trial.
www.smugglersnotchdistillery.com

STONECUTTER SPIRITS

Middlebury

Founders Sas Stewart and Sivan Cotel are not only passionate about good aged gin, but they are also creative with whiskey. It is distilled "like a bourbon in Kentucky, then brought to Vermont to age in a process similar to that of Irish whiskey, then finished in the same way as certain premium scotch. With American gins, to be called a gin, you need juniper—but beyond that, you can add any number of botanicals or spices that you want. Some people get a little crazy and add twenty to thirty different spices; some people will go super-dry and just have juniper and citrus," Stewart said. "For us, we wanted to think first about how we could age a gin." They create their gin recipe around the flavors of the bourbon barrels and express flavors such as vanillas, caramels, oak, and bourbon. "The gin is infused with botanicals including cardamom, orange peel, green tea, coriander, licorice root, and even rose petals. The Single Barrel Gin sports a much paler hue than a lot of aged gins we've seen, reflecting its soft aging approach."
www.stonecutterspirits.com

Vermont Distillers

Guilford

Founded in 2012 by Ed Metcalfe, Vermont Distillers produces Maple Cream Liqueur, made using fine Vermont maple syrup, fresh cream, and fine spirits. A family-run company, Ed joins his sons, Augustus and Dominic, whom he raised with a passion for Vermont maple syrup. The trio work together to constantly come up with innovative products.

Before founding Vermont Distillers, Metcalfe was the owner and creator of the North River Winery, Vermont's first winery, which he started in 1985 and sold in 1997 to pursue other ventures.

Along with the flagship product, Metcalfe's Vermont Maple Cream Liqueur, Vermont Distillers produces Metcalfe's Vermont Maple Liqueur and Metcalfe's Raspberry Liqueur.

www.vermontdistillers.com

Vermont Spirits Co.

Quechee

"We employ a variety of custom stills to create our line of spirits," noted Steve Johnson, owner of Vermont Spirits Co. "We typically begin with our stripping still, which is a large stainless box with a series of protruding condensers, making it look like something from a Dr. Seuss book," he continued. "Next, we either go to our one-of-a-kind 150-gallon copper pot still, or one of our two glass fractionating columns, ordinarily used in industrial continuous flow stills, to complete our batch-distilling process. A fractionating column distillation is the most accurate way to isolate and separate impurities, leaving the most flavorful and smoothest alcohol from the 'heart of the run.'"

The Vermont Gold is their flagship product, though the bourbon and barrel-aged cocktails are very popular with clientele, as well. As for personal favorites, Johnson said, "The vodka. I love vodka tonics. We recently reformulated the gin, the goal is an American style gin, and it's been doing well."

Local sourcing is important, and the juniper in the gin comes from northern Vermont. The crew picks enough in the spring to get them through the year.

What's new for 2017 and 2018? "[We] want to keep the apple brandy going. Apples got pretty expensive recently," said Johnson.

Stills tend to be unique in Vermont. "Our main still employs a converted maple arch, which is a flat, shallow pan used to concentrate maple syrup," Johnson explained. "We've got some designs in the works to basically triple the size. We like the shallow pan because it gives us more control. Maple is expensive, and we need to get everything out of it we can."

Johnson, like many others, looks to European oak for barrels. He said, "The apple brandy we age in new Hungarian oak barrels. We might finish in a bourbon barrel. The whiskey and the aged cocktails are aged in new American oak barrels."

One of the more unusual products is their vodka. "I think a lot of people will be intrigued by a vodka made from milk (sugar)," Johnson said. "We've been making this for a while, and now there are several others in the United States as well. It was a challenge to get it right."

Johnson added, "Being in Vermont has a been a big help. There are many craft distilleries now, and Vermont has a reputation for having great apples, maple, and pure water. We're glad to help add to the state."
www.vermontspirits.com

While in Quechee, stop at the bridge over the Ottauquechee River to view Quechee Gorge, known as "Vermont's Little Grand Canyon." Experience it up close walking the trail along the mile-long chasm.

WHISTLEPIG WHISKEY

Middlebury

WhistlePig was founded by Raj Bhakta in 2007, but the story began long before that when Bhakta appeared on the TV show *The Apprentice* and was famously "fired" by Trump. That was followed by a second disappointment—losing a race for the US congress in 2006, during which he rode an elephant across the Rio Grande accompanied by a mariachi band to show the state of border security. So Bhakta purchased the 500-acre Vermont farm and pursued his dream of creating aged rye whiskey.

As stated on the WhistlePig Whiskey website, "Raj was a single malt Scotch fan. And patriotic. He felt like America should have the best whiskey in the world. And, after having rye whiskey, decided that was it. Fortunately, Raj ran into Master Distiller Dave Pickerell, who had just left Maker's Mark and had a great stash of Canadian rye that he was having trouble selling in the United States. It was the best rye Raj had ever tasted, and so he and Dave worked to blend and bottle the first WhistlePig."

The 10 Year is WhistlePig's flagship release—100-proof, straight rye whiskey, aged for at least ten years through a unique double-barrel process. The 10 Year has bold, spicy rye notes that earned a 96-point rating from *Wine Enthusiast* magazine.

Bhakta enjoys all of his brand's offerings, but said, "The Boss Hog Independent is out of this world."

What's new for 2017 and 2018? FarmStock, a triple terroir whiskey. This momentous undertaking sets the stage for the upcoming release of WhistlePig triple terroir whiskeys in the future. To achieve triple terroir, every part of creating the whiskey happens on the farm "right up until the moment the liquid is bottled," Bhakta noted. This means using on-site water together with rye grain grown on the farm, and aging the whiskey in barrels constructed from wood grown on the property.

Like most stills, the one at WhistlePig has its own story. The unique copper pot still was designed by Dave Pickerell. "Dave has been involved in the design of hundreds of distilleries. This was the culmination of his experience and was designed as a pure rye distillery," Bhakta noted.

"Vermont is about as far north as oak trees can grow. The shorter growing season leads to oak trees with the tightest rings. Why is this important? When aging whiskey encounters a ring in a barrel, it imparts greater flavor, so our custom Vermont oak barrels bring tremendous depth to our whiskeys," explained Pickerell. "One more reason to love Vermont.

"We're experimenting with four or five years. The flavor is imparting more profoundly and quickly. More flavor, since the trees are older and they struggle more in this climate. The wood has more character to give, so it comes out faster.

"There is no more flavorful whiskey than rye. The bad news? Rye is stubborn and robust. It has spicy character, and a dark, rich flavor. To attain a signature smoothness, rye must be aged longer than other whiskies. Rye isn't sweet. In fact, it contains less sugar than any other grain. The challenges involved in producing rye whiskey are many. But when handled properly, there is no comparison: the brat rye whiskey, once tamed, emerges from many years in the barrel with the power of a linebacker and the grace of a ballerina. We grow all of our rye grain right here on our farm. As for the spent grain, we feed it to our pigs. The pork then becomes part of the menu for guests.

"The most extraordinary two things about WhistlePig are one, our ambitions and aspirations are coming from a small farm in Vermont to have the single finest whiskey label in the world, and two, we are looking to achieve that through harvesting the full potential of our farm here, [using elements from the whole farm in the process] in Vermont. Nobody else is doing that. Our grain, our water, our wood. So, on the one hand, we have global aspirations, and on the other, we have deep roots here on our farm in Vermont."

www.whistlepigwhiskey.com

A wind has blown the rain away and blown
the sky away and all the leaves away,
and the trees stand. I think, i too, have known
autumn too long.

—e. e. cummings

CIDERIES

It isn't hard to see that apples were important to early settlers in Vermont. Almost every old farm you come across here has an orchard somewhere near the farmhouse. Making cider was a good way to preserve apples not used for fresh eating or cooking, and the alcohol produced ensured it was sanitary.

While Vermont's cider traditions took a big hit during Prohibition, orcharding has remained an important part of the agricultural economy here. Modern commercial orchards don't grow most of the thousands of varieties that were once commonplace, but the cider renaissance is starting to change that. Piggybacking on an already strong tradition of craft food here in Vermont, cider makers and orchardists here are looking to the past for inspiration but are excited to write a new chapter in the history of Vermont apple growing. —Colin Davis, Cofounder, Shacksbury Cider

CITIZEN CIDER

Burlington

Justin Heilenbach, Bryan Holmes, and Kris Nelson founded Citizen Cider in 2010 "on a hunch and some good old-fashioned hard work," according to Nelson. Kris was working as a wine salesman, Bryan as a chemist, and Justin as a small farmer. "All of us were discontent for one reason or another," so they started pressing sweet cider in Nelson's barn and fermenting test batches of hard cider in Holmes' basement. "As it happens," Nelson said, "[we] discovered that [our] ideas about hard cider translated into some pretty unique and interesting finished products."

"I was selling wine for a wholesaler when I read Michael Pollan's book *The Botany of Desire*," Nelson said. "I was struck by the section about apples and cider and how fundamental they were to the interaction between food and culture in this country. It really struck me: here we were in Vermont with all these apples and history, the local craft beer scene was blossoming, but, except for Woodchuck, there wasn't as much going on with cider. How could this have disappeared? How could we go from a place where cider was one of the primary beverages to being virtually nonexistent?"

He continued, "Justin, Bryan, and I started talking. There was a craft cider scene starting up in Portland, and we wondered if we could make craft cider here. We found a local community of homecrafted cider makers and some small crafted artisanal ciders, but there wasn't much cider to consume on premises. Except for Woodchuck, cider wasn't a big part of the drinking scene in the Northeast."

They found a homemade, large wooden apple press on Craigslist. "We brought it to my barn and cleaned it up. [We] started gathering apples from a variety of orchards and became friends with Stan and Mary [Pratt], who own Happy Valley Orchards in Middlebury, Vermont," Nelson said.

"We wanted to make a cider that was appealing to everyone, which was where we came up with the name Citizen Cider. We wanted to make an accessible cider for the people," he explained. "We wanted to help bring people into the cider category by making a semidry product, which is our Unified Press." The company's flagship beverage, United Press, is made from 100 percent locally sourced apples. The name came from the fact that the three of them were centered around cider, united around it using the old press.

Nelson said, "We built this business from the ground up, and relatively quickly. Around here we have what we call 'cider years' (similar to dog years), one calendar year is about five cider years."

As for a personal favorite, Nelson said, "I'm all over the place. Unified Press, I go back to that a lot. Lately I've been enjoying the Wit's Up, a dry cider that goes through malolactic fermentation, which makes it super approachable and gives it an ale like mouthfeel. The Brosé is good, too; drinks like a rosé from southern France. We made about forty different ciders over the course of the year."

What's new for 2017 and 2018? "The restaurant and tasting room are always evolving. There's a broad spectrum of visitors we cater to. There's a large group of local young people, there's the people exploring the craft beer scene who stumble upon us, and there are the cider lovers. The restaurant is comfy, we serve comfort food. There are mountain views and outdoor seating. We feel like we belong here and we're a part of the community," Nelson said. "We're constantly trying to up our game to serve food that goes with cider. We're evolving and pushing new styles. Different yeasts and fermentation styles. There's a trend toward drier styles."

Citizen Cider is currently distributed in all New England states, New York City, and parts of upstate New York, North and South Carolina, and Illinois.

Nelson said, "Some ciders are only available at the tasting room, either on draft or bottled. One of our oaked ciders is called Mr. Burlington; it's kind of an old-fashioned cocktail style with bitters and orange peel."

Many of the ciders are orchard-specific: "We work with a handful of orchards in Vermont and New York. We feel like both states have the same apple-growing ecosystem," noted Nelson.

"There is a terroir-driven difference. We do a few orchard-specific ciders, for example Stan Up from the Happy Valley Orchard. It's an interesting place; Stan has fifty-five different varieties of apples there. We also did a pressing with the heirloom apples from the grounds of the Shelburne Museum," Nelson said. "We did an exclusive cider for Whole Foods that used apples from Wayne County, New York."

As for labeling ciders as vintage, Nelson commented, "The Stan Up is labeled as a vintage. We will be expanding vintages a little; creating ciders that people can lay down and age. It's harder to isolate geographic cider characteristics than it is in wine, but we're thinking about it. It's interesting, even though cider is so old, the science and art of fermentation is still breaking ground. And there are still so many varieties of apples that we could grow here. We're at the very beginning."

The Lake Hopper product "is made entirely with apples and cascade hops from the same landscape, and in some cases the same farms, this cider is a tribute to those things that connect us. Two States. One Landscape. One Cider," said Nelson.

This cider is aged in reclaimed oak bourbon barrels. "We take our finest cider blends, let them sit in these American oak barrels, and while they get to know each other, a beautiful relationship emerges," Nelson said. These products are "best enjoyed with a big steak and a friend."

The barrels come from oak that has been aged in spent bourbon. "And we have done a few experiments with rum barrels," Nelson said. "Cider is different from spirits, wines, or beers, it embraces whatever flavors it encounters. Very quickly. You put cider into a new oak barrel and you taste oak."

Local products are important to Citizen Cider, and they use 100 percent locally sourced apples and cider for 100 percent of their products, 100 percent of the time.

Nelson added, "Our model for craft cider is that we use whole apples, never from concentrate, there's no added sugar, and we work directly with growers. We're having a positive impact on the local economy. We feel really good about what we are doing."
www.citizencider.com

Eden Specialty Ciders

Newport

Eden's specialty ciders speak to the apple heritage of Vermont and the cold winter climate of the region. Their ciders are innovative and interesting, and their philosophy is to honor the rare, valuable apples that they are fortunate enough to use. Eden does this by using natural techniques rather than industrial ones that a large producer might use, which often can aggressively manipulate the fruit.

"We work with traditional New England heirloom varieties, local seedling varieties, and Old World varieties, including bittersweet cider varieties that originated in France and England. We press once per year after harvest. We use the natural winter cold at our farm to concentrate the flavors and sugars of the apples before fermentation. The highest concentrated juice we use to make our famed Eden Ice Ciders. It takes over eight pounds of apples to make one 375ml bottle of ice cider! Lesser concentrations form the base for our Orleans aperitifs and our naturally sparkling ciders. We never use sugar, colorings, acids, or industrial flavorings in our ciders," the website states.

All of the apples are estate grown at the Eden Orchards, located in the Northeast Kingdom. "Our greatest pleasure as cider makers is working with the extraordinary apples we have in our region and the people who grow them," the owners state on the website.

Eden Orchards uses a practice developed by Rudolph Steiner called biodynamics, in which everything in the production process must derive from the farm, be produced naturally, and follow complex lunar cycles.

Eden has a strong relationship with its growers and is in several long-term partnerships to access the best fruit possible. "Together we cope with what Mother Nature provides in the way of weather and help each other to insure quality fruit and quality ciders. When you buy our ciders, you are supporting all of us and our working landscape," their website noted.

"Everyone on our little team plays a key role in delivering a wonderful cider experience for our customers. We work hard, we have fun, and we love our families, our landscape, and our community."
www.edenciders.com

FLAG HILL FARM

Vershire

Flag Hill produces traditional farmhouse-style Vermont hard cyders, as well as distilled fruit spirits, Pomme-de-Vie and Stair's Pears, which they refer to as "Vermont brandies." The farm has been organic since 1984, and is Certified Organic.

The farm's sparking and still cyders are made in small batches. They spell it with a Y to "distinguish our handmade farmhouse product from apple cider and mass-marketed carbonated apple 'wines,'" explains the farm's website.

Flag Hill's sparkling Vermont Cyder is aged for two years and then fermented in the bottle. The Still Hard Cyder is made from wild and cultivated tart cider apples and aged in barrels for two years. The newest addition to the lineup is Sapsucker, an extra-dry Belgian beer-style hard cyder.

The cyders are available only in Vermont by limited release and are packaged in hand-numbered bottles. *www.flaghillfarm.com*

SHACKSBURY CIDER

Vergennes

Shacksbury is dedicated to sourcing the best apples in the region, and the staff has worked diligently to find them through a rigorous process of sampling from thousands of apples. They have fermented ciders from over 150 unique trees and ultimately selected twelve varieties to propagate. "We have grafted these twelve varieties to over 1,000 trees, marking the beginning of our 'Lost Apple Orchard' at co-owner Colin Davis's farm and with our partners, Sunrise Orchards and Windfall Orchard. Each year we continue to harvest, graft, and plant trees in an effort to expand our source of Lost Apples," wrote cofounder David Dolginow.

"Far from ordinary," continued Dolginow, "apples are the most diverse food plant on earth. Unfortunately, only a handful of varieties are cultivated at scale in America, and all of those are designed for eating, not cider making."

Shacksbury's philosophy is that cider can, and should, be "daring and complex." "From gnarled trees on New England farmsteads to Old World orchards in England and Spain, our cider will change the way you think about this amazing fruit," wrote Dolginow.

What makes Shacksbury so special is its true dedication to the history and heritage of cidering in Vermont. "The apples of America's early cider tradition," wrote Dolginow, were "lost for a variety of reasons, are not hard to find in Vermont—once you know what you're looking for. Though far less numerous than they once were, the trees materialize around every bend, and over every hill, hiding in plain sight. To us, these trees represent a door to another time, and are the basis for superior cider." *www.shacksbury.com*

Stowe Cider

Stowe

"Mark Ray jumped right into the industry when Stowe Cider owners Stefan and Mary Windler hired him to manage the business. He became Cider Certified through the United States Association of Cider Makers and has been involved with production of all Stowe Cider products since joining the company," said tasting room manager, Nikki Nizynski.

Stowe Cider's flagship product is Tips Up, a semidry, apple-forward cider with a gorgeous balance and big McIntosh flavor.

What's new for 2017 and 2018? "We have big plans for 2017! We are entering three new markets: New York City, Washington, DC, and Connecticut for the first time, in addition to continuing to expand our current presence in Vermont and Massachusetts. We will be expanding into a larger production site this summer, with the tasting room following later during the year as well," commented the excited Nizynski. "This will allow us to not only keep up with distribution demands, but also bring the tasting room and production under one roof again. We will be able to build a tour program, and guests will be able to witness cider being made while they enjoy their flights."

Many customers describe their ciders as "the Best Around," and the awards certainly lean in that direction.

At Stowe Cider, "we like to think outside the box, so you never know what we'll come up with next! For example, last year we collaborated with four Vermont distilleries to incorporate their spent gin botanicals in our cider," said Nizynski.

"We have supporters who have been there since day one and come back to Stowe or come into the tasting room regularly to fill growlers and see how much we've grown. At the same time, the introduction to new markets plus our current tasting room location right in the heart of Stowe brings newcomers every day," continued Nizynski. "We like to think of them as regulars waiting to happen."

While Stowe Cider doesn't currently have a sour program, they have done a wild fermented cider in the past, and don't rule it out for the future.

Several of its annual winter release ciders are barrel aged, and some of the seasonal ciders may be aged as well. "With the number of distilleries around us, we have access to a variety of barrels and plan on continuing to foster those great relationships so that we can keep the barrel-aged ciders coming," Nizynski added.

Stowe Cider uses 100 percent locally sourced apples, primarily from the Champlain Valley and central Vermont. They typically use a blend of apples, the favorite being the McIntosh and other dessert apple varietals. "Whenever we incorporate an herb, fruit, or any other ingredient in our cider, we focus on partnering with our local neighboring farms," she noted.

"We have a mix of filtered and unfiltered ciders, depending on the style and how we chose to package that particular one," remarked Nizynski. "Our cider is unpasteurized, and most of our cider includes pitched yeast, but we have done wild ciders in the past and wouldn't rule out the possibility of doing so again."
www.stowecider.com

WOODCHUCK CIDER

Middlebury

John Matson was a brewer who took the traditional route, attending brewing school in Chicago, after which he started working at Otter Creek Brewing until it was purchased. He then held several positions at Woodchuck Cider, ultimately migrating to his current position in product development.

Woodchuck's flagship beverage is the Amber, the company's original cider which is described as "a refreshing red apple Amber. . . . Fiercely crafted with a medium body, golden hue, and refreshing red apple finish."

Matson's personal favorite of the ciders they make year-round is the Semidry. It's made from "a nice blend of European cider fruit and North American table varieties," he noted.

What's new for 2017 and 2018? "We're always doing something new in the cider room," Matson said. "As far as cider, we've recently changed the summer cider formulation. Under the Gumption label we do our Late Show. It's a rotating variety of ciders that comes out four to six times a year. For example, we'll have a chocolate cider, a cranberry honey, and a grapefruit-infused cider."

Matson said, "I think people like us because we were the first craft cider producer in the United States. We created the market. We also started innovating early and have continued to expand the category. From time to time we'll put together firkins and kegs; special one-offs at the cider house. If there's an event, I'll blend up something special for sampling."

As for Woodchuck's Hopsation, they start with small batch hard cider that is then infused with Cascade hops to "impart sensational pine and citrus aromas," said Matson. "The smooth apple character of our signature hard cider balances perfectly against the bitterness of the hops. Some may just call it a 'hopsational' cider."

The barrels are purchased through brokers and come from wineries in California and from distilleries in Kentucky.

Amber is a mix of apple varieties. Matson noted, "The majority of our apples are from the table varieties that you find in stores. I like brewing with some of the European varieties, but there aren't that many acres planted since a grower gets three times as much per bushel for table-quality fruit as the culled ones used in cider. We do a lot of blending to get a consistent product for people. We have a set range for acidity and sugar, and we adjust the blend to get there."

Matson said, "We are working with the University of Vermont and Barney [Hodges] out at Sunrise Orchards. We've dedicated some resources to plant an orchard of cider fruit. We're also looking at alternative orcharding techniques: spraying the fruit less and managing the orchard less than they would for table-quality fruit. Then maybe we could pay a little more for cider fruit and he would have better margins since his costs are lower. It's a long-term project."

Matson explained how some of the process works: "After the base cider fermentation is done, we use a cross-flow filter. (If you're a guy who knows his filters, you know that's pretty good.) Later on, a set of membrane filters is used to achieve a really darn high level of purity. This is one of the reasons Woodchuck has such a long shelf life. We now pasteurize our products. We used to use potassium sorbate to help stabilize the cider, but we don't need that anymore. We use Champagne yeast, since it's a killer yeast. We don't need sulfites in the fermenter. Cider is pressed at a local farm. The pomace is used as fertilizer and for feed supplements."

Matson concluded, "One of the cool things about us is that we've been doing it for so long. That's all we do. Cider isn't just a revenue stream for us, it's what we are, it's who we are. And the way we help push the category forward, we also push it for other craft cider makers as well."

www.woodchuck.com

Dust of Snow
The way a crow
Shook down on me
The dust of snow
From a hemlock tree

Has given my heart
A change of mood
And saved some part
Of a day I had rued.

—Robert Frost

BREWERIES

Vermont's brewers are an independent group. Each beer and brewery has its own unique story and distinct style. Yet the camaraderie among brewers found in the industry is found in great strength here too, where brewers willingly share brewing techniques and ingredients readily with one another in the pursuit of making the best beer possible. For me, the Vermont Brewers Association, our state guild, has developed one of the better synopses of why Vermont beer is special.

Vermonters have a deep respect for what's genuine, and an aversion to anything that falls short. Vermont didn't become one of the world's most respected beer destinations overnight. It took a generation of pioneers who are revered by the state's brewers today, and a new breed of innovators. We don't dumb down our beers for the mass market. Because we're putting our name on something much bigger than our name. Wherever you go in Vermont, you'll find different styles, different tastes, and a common bond. And with every new taste, you'll get to know the flavor of our state a little better. From the brewers who led the way, establishing our craft, to a new generation of taprooms waiting to be discovered. In Vermont, our search for the perfect pint is fueled by a passionate and inquisitive spirit. We explore further and dig deeper. All so that we can create a beer unlike anyone else. —Sean Lawson, Owner, Lawson's Finest Liquids

1ST REPUBLIC BREWING CO.

Essex Junction

1st Republic Brewing Co. was started in a garage by friends Kevin Jarvis and Shawn Trout, both military veterans. With a strong tradition and history in Vermont, the company was founded to "honor this nation's first republic." While they maintain "an eye for the future," they always note the breweries connection to history as well.

As they state on the company website: "1st Republic Brewing Co. has deep Vermont roots and represents the heart and soul of the hardworking people of this great state." Stop by the taproom in Essex, Vermont, to get a taste of the results of their hard work, which includes Ardent Concession IPA, French Saison, Shifting Specifics, and their newest addition, Ceres Brown Ale. *www.1strepublicbrewingco.com*

14TH STAR BREWING

St. Albans

Vermonter and beer enthusiast, Ethan Allen was a leader in the effort to make Vermont the fourteenth star on the US flag in the year 1791. It is said that Allen often drank beer at a local Inn in Vermont. In honor of Allen's history, and the long brewing traditions of the state, 14th Star Brewing's owner, Army veteran Steve Gagner, created 14th Star Brewing.

14th Star is Gagner's 1,200-square-foot nano brewery in St. Albans, currently producing small-batch offerings in approximately 900 gallons, or twenty-eight barrels, of beer each month.

What makes 14th Star's beers stand out? Well, the care with which "we handle our beer throughout the brewing process, coupled with our desire to brew the best beer humanly possible," wrote Gagner. Additionally, 14th Star has a clear dedication to the Vermont beer community and the local community they take part in as well. "We understand that we are part of a tradition of brewing fantastic beer here in Vermont, and our goal is to continue to push the bar higher. But that's not it. Not entirely," said Gagner. "You see—at this size, we can brew whatever we want to brew, without the shackles of order fulfillment from a large distributor. In nine months, we've brewed a Pale Ale, a Honey IPA (with honey sourced from right here in Franklin County), a Cascade IPA, a Golden Wheat, a Roasted Porter, an Amber Ale (Valor), a Citrus APA (1493), a Brown Ale, and a Winter Warmer. These beers pop into our rotation as we get the itch to brew them."

What makes their beer special is that they let their imaginations run free as they brew beers that are unique to the area, and serve a niche clientele. *www.14thstarbrewing.com*

BACKACRE BEERMAKERS

Weston

A small producer, Backacre Beermakers focuses on one product: a sour golden ale that is aged for more than a year in oak barrels. To create the beer's earthy, fruity, and tart flavor, they utilize a mix of cultures, rather than a single yeast strain, along with blending, a very old practice that is still used in some areas of Belgium and Germany. Backacre works in concert with local brewers to produce wort, or unfermented beer, which Backacre ferments, and then blends the beer from different barrels to provide the balance of flavors they desire.
www.backacrebeermakers.com

BENT HILL BREWERY

Braintree

Bent Hill Brewery produces a series of diverse ales. The brewery's dedication to local ingredients is a characteristic found in many artisanal breweries in Vermont. What sets Bent Hill apart is the water, which comes from an on-site well and helps create a unique flavor, and the fact that some of the ingredients used are from their own land. They grow hops, blackberries, blueberries, currants, and cherries. Beers include Hoppy Table Saison, Double Dry Hopped Blood Orange Double IPA, Smoked Sea Salt Caramel Coconut Porter, Maple Red, and Chocolate Ginger Carrot Stout.
www.benthillbrewery.com

BOBCAT CAFÉ AND BREWERY

Bristol

Owners Erin and Sanderson Wheeler create roughly a dozen different offerings at Bobcat Café and Brewery, located in the heart of the Green Mountains. They use high-quality local ingredients, such as hops, grains, and yeast, to experiment with flavor while upholding each beer's distinctive traditional character.

Stop in for a bucket of wings and a pint of one of the house beers, such as Blonde, Prayer Rock Pale Ale, or Nut Brown.
www.thebobcatcafe.com

BREWSTER RIVER PUB AND BREWERY

Jeffersonville

Just a hop and a skip from Smugglers' Notch, the Brewster River Pub and Brewery offers thirteen of Vermont's best beers on tap. This selection includes three made in-house: Dunkelweizen, Barrel Fermented Saison, and Vanilla Bourbon Porter. Their motto is "Beer, Burgers & BBQ," and Brewster's is a great place for all three.
www.brewsterriverpubnbrewery.com

BROCKLEBANK CRAFT BREWING

Tunbridge

Located in Tunbridge, Vermont, at the site of a former dairy farm, Brocklebank Craft Brewing focuses on seasonal offerings and traditional hop-forward beers with creative local flavors. Classified as a one-and-a-half barrel nano brewery, supply is short and demand more than matches this.

Ben Linehan, owner and brewer, began brewing in 2009 and has garnered quite a bit of acclaim. Beers include hoppy American pale ales and German and Czech styles. *www.brocklebankvt.com*

BURLINGTON BEER CO.

Williston

Established in 2014, Burlington Beer Company is known for its use of local and international malts, hops, yeast, fruit, vegetables, spices, and herbs. Founder Joe Lemnah had plenty of experience, working at Olde Saratoga Brewing Co., Dogfish Head Craft Brewing Co., and Evolution Craft Brewing Co. before returning to Vermont and then starting his own brewery.

Always balancing between tradition and innovation, Burlington Beer Company's taproom is a fantastic spot to visit. *www.burlingtonbeercompany.com*

DROP-IN BREWING CO.

Middlebury

Drop-In Brewing Company, located in a former plumbing supply building on Route 7 South in Middlebury, features a tasting room, complete with growlers. It is also home of the American Brewers Guild Brewing School (www.abgbrew.com), which brewery owners Steve Parkes and Christine McKeever-Parkes purchased in the early 2000s.

The breweries flagship product is Sunshine & Hoppiness, which is described on the brewery's website as "light and crisp with delicious Belgian flavors that balance perfectly with American Cascade hops." Additional offerings include the Scottish-inspired Heart of Lothian, with hints of chocolate and caramel, and Red Dwarf, an American amber ale.

www.dropinbrewing.com

Vermont is known for cows, but it's also home to The UVM Morgan Horse Farm, located just north of Middlebury in Weybridge, Vermont. The farm is dedicated to the preservation of the Morgan horse, America's first breed of horse, and is home to significant Morgan history.

FARNHAM ALE & LAGER

South Burlington

Farnham Ale & Lager opened its South Burlington location in 2015, where it offers a combination of year-round and seasonal brews, pub food, entertainment, and a spacious taproom. Its mission: making craft beer accessible to all.

Founded by Alex Jacob, known to be a man of few words, Farnham Ale's success is based on its winning team. The original Farnham Ale & Lager is located in Farnham, Quebec, where Jacob, a native of Quebec, has a number of restaurants and bars. He wanted to expand and tried to import his beers to Maine, but instead found an opportunity in Burlington, Vermont. When he hired all locals, they took the foundation of Farnham and put a Vermont spin on it.

Avery Lemnah, who started in September 2016, is one of the happy employees. "I went to school for athletic training and was working as a chiropractor. I wasn't happy there and felt there was something more.

"I love beer, the brewing side, and the tasting side," Lemnah continued. "I stumbled upon Farnham when they started in 2015, and I fell in love with the image of it. 'I am going to come back once a week until I have a job with you' [I told them]. A year later, I got the job."

Beers have an IBU number, and Lemnah, who enjoys the educational aspect of the brewery, likes it when someone asks her about the number. "Then they are getting educated," she said. "I get to then tell them what IBUs are. [IBU stands for the International Bitterness Unit scale.] Our double IPA is seventy-eight. I use the analogy of a sleep number bed, so you get to figure out what you like. If you don't like bitter, never grab a beer over thirty-five."

Brewer Kendall Kreds considers his role to be simple. "I brew the beer. I stay out of the taproom because I screw everything up," he said. "I have been brewing since October 2015. I wasn't a professional brewer before that. I was an avid homebrewer."

Kreds, who has a background in microbiology, originally applied for the taproom manager position, since he thought they would want a professional brewer. "However," Kreds said, "they wanted someone who knew how to brew but wasn't a professional. They wanted to teach the person how to brew."

As for a beer-making philosophy, Kreds's main goal is to "make it reproducible. We want to make a drinkable beer that is affordable and accessible to the vast majority of people in Vermont. We want to produce a solid line of beers. We aren't going to be doing exotic things (like fruits to beers). But for each style we make—while it is more traditional—they all include our own twist. But we want to make great, solid beer."

Jacob said, "We let Vermont influence the beer. The Quebec palate likes maltiness over bitterness. Malt is from the grain, bitter is from the hops. In Quebec, when you order an IPA, it looks like a brown ale. In Vermont, the hoppier the better. A few of our beers are very similar, but different because of the water. Our small batches are unique to Vermont. We made our beers hazier, hoppier, and move to a more robust aroma. We are trying to learn from the locals and go from there."

Farnham began with four core drinks: #12 Hefeweizen beer; #35 Bitter, a classic pub ale; #42, Session IPA, a lighter beer typically brewed in the summer; and #58 IPA.

What customers say is that their beer has the hue of a Hefeweizen and the proper banana flavor.

Kreds has a favorite, of course, and it is #65 Russian Imperial Stout, a darker, heavier beer. "We made a small batch. We are almost out. I might be a little biased, because I know the work that went into making it. I appreciate it a little bit more," he said. "Standard brew, when you mash/mill the grain, you add to the heated water. When you extract the sugars to make the sugars fermentable. This is usually a one-step process. With stout, you do this process twice with two different types of grains. Because it is a bigger, bolder beer, you need lots of grains to get all the sugars you need. Once fermentation is done, then the stout was aged in bourbon barrels. We tried the beer every week until we liked the flavor. We then pumped the beer out of the barrels and carbonated them and then bottled them."

What is new for 2017 and 2018? "We are going to be bringing in a few food trucks that give people a variety of food. We are going to be experimenting with different beers and doing small batches. We started with doing what we knew well with big batches. The year 2017 brings more experiments. We are going to be doing some lighter, crisper beers in the summer, including a pilsner. Our next release is a red lager. We are expanding from dark beers to lighter spring beers. I am excited to get the garage doors open and bring in fresh air to the brewery and get the live music going. Burlington gets busier in the summer. I am excited to have this brewery be a part of that Burlington atmosphere," said Jacob.

All the grains they use are from Country Malt Group from across the lake in New York, and they source their hops from a company in Oregon. The spent grain is given to Pine Island Farms, a goat farm in Colchester.

Farnham's customers "like that we are not trying to do anything extreme. We believe in good-quality, stable beer. It is drinkable. It's not crazy. They can go through an entire flight and not hate a single one. Even if they like lighter beers, they will still like the stout," said Jacob. "If people really like IPAs, they will still like the Hefeweizen. People will swear against IPAs, and then they will really like their IPA. We make people rethink their personal tastes."
www.farnham-alelager.com

FIDDLEHEAD BREWING CO.

Shelburne

Fiddlehead Brewing Company produces full-flavored beers "with the true beer connoisseur in mind." The brewery sources locally, and the beers' depth of flavor certainly comes from the fresh ingredients that Vermont offers.

Matthew Cohen (known industrywide as Matty O) is on his own self-proclaimed "continual quest to craft the perfect pint." Fiddlehead's flagship beer, Fiddlehead IPA, is popular in restaurants and bars throughout the state.
www.fiddleheadbrewing.com

FOAM BREWERS

Burlington

In the early-1990s, Todd Haire was working in a beer store and was fascinated with craft beer. "Then I started home brewing and really wanted to pursue my passion more professionally. I begged for a job in Hoboken and worked for free at a small brewery on Hudson and 11th Street. It was in the days that craft beer was so young. It was either an amber ale or a golden ale. I didn't see myself working there in the long term. Beer gave me an outlet to be do something interesting," Haire said.

"Then I came back to Vermont and applied for and received the Michael Jackson Beer Education Scholarship (Michael Jackson the beer writer from England, not the King of Pop), through the American Institute of Wine & Food," Haire continued. With the scholarship, he went to the Siebel Institute of Technology in Chicago. "I was there in 1996 and 1997 with Bradley Coors and Jennifer Yuengling (of Yuengling Brewery, the oldest brewery in the country). I got a diploma in brewing."

Haire's friend, Paul Sayler, let him know that Magic Hat was expanding and looking for a brewer. It had only been around for a few of years at that time. "My wife and I moved up to Vermont in April 1998, and I spent about thirteen years overseeing brewing operations and growing. The brewery went from a small local brewery, producing 2,000 barrels a year, to 180,000 barrels a year, the ninth largest craft brewery in the country during the time Todd was brewing there," said Sayler.

When the management shifted at Magic Hat, Haire took the opportunity to move on. He went across town to Switchback Brewing Company, where he spent four years as a head brewer.

During that time, Haire hired two people, Robert Grim and Sam Keane. Together, the trio brought in additional partners and formed Foam.

"It's a great group that we were able to pull together and make great beer," Haire said. "We all shared the same idea: we wanted to continue to be creative, make interesting beers, put some humanity into it, and give people a place to enjoy themselves in a relaxed atmosphere and have fun. We control everything, from severing it to the music that is played."

The inspiration for making beer comes to the Foam group "from everything from music to food, to the staff that likes to have input. We stay on top of how beer is evolving, but at the end of the day, it's about what we enjoy. We like to take risks, try new things and see what happens. People enjoy the creativity of our beers," added Haire.

Many customers enjoy the mixed-culture beers, which tend to be the company's most creative beers. "We aren't making what I call 'peanut butter beers,' where we add

wacky flavors for the sake of being different. We just did a beer called 'The Influence of Heat,' an imperial milk stout (9 percent) that had vanilla beans," Haire said. "Brio, a local coffee roaster, would get four different types of roasts for us, and we would do a taste with the beer, and then brew the beer with the chosen roast."

In addition, Foam has a 10 barrel (500-gallon tanks) that has a woody foeder. The foeder is an oak vessel. "We brewed a beer that has a mixed culture (regular yeast, wild yeast, and saison yeast, and lactic acid which gives tartness). We got the foeder, then added 350 pounds of Montmorency cherries (pits and all) from New York," Haire continued.

Another unique aspect of Foam is that it is situated in an 1850s mill factory. "We wanted to create a nice place for people to drink beer. With a nice place to enjoy conversation and enjoy great beer and small charcuterie plates. We don't believe in TVs," Haire said.

The name was selected because "Everything a brewer works for is to have a great head on beer. It sounds great, and because we are right on the water," Haire continued. "We brought all those influences to the brewery. Foam Brewery is a reflection of great beer. Every great beer should be capped with a great head of foam. It drives the aroma and taste."

For something different and nonalcoholic, Foam carries a small

Meat pies available for sale at the Foam taproom.

local vendor that creates Queen City Kombucha Urban Latte, and Brio does cold-pressed coffee on nitrogen.

As for a personal favorite, Haire loves Pavement. "I am also a huge fan of the pilsner, Tranquil Pils."

What's new for 2017 and 2018? "We have a lot of different foeder beers and wood-aged beers that we are going to be doing. We also are exploring new IPAs with new hop varieties and continuing to evolve some of our saisons," Haire replied.

"We have a three-step process. We brew it. We ferment it. We serve it. We don't keg anything," remarked Haire.

One of Foam's side projects is the House of Fermentology. That project started a year before Foam and is focused on fermenting and aging beers in wooden barrels.

The brewery sources locally and brews some of their beers with local honey. Haire explained, "I have about five [bee] colonies and can add seventy-five pounds of honey. We did a sleepy time beer that had lemon zest and chamomile.

All of our base malt, 90 percent of our malt, we use Peterson Quality Malt, which is right out of Monkton, Vermont. All the barley comes from Vermont and he malts it in the malt house. We use 100 percent of his malted barley for our beers. We use [hops from] the University of Vermont . . . the hops they grow through their extension (Nugget, Chinook, Cascade)."

The spent grain is used to feed local dairy cows and pigs. The farmer picks it up two or three times a week.

Customers love visiting Foam, which draws a mixture of locals and tourists alike. "Burlington has a huge student population, but we still get a mix. Our crowds [range in age from] twenty-five to sixty years old. People like that our beers are dry, flavorful, aromatic, and creative. The beer is important," Haire said, "but the atmosphere where everyone is sitting and relaxing makes the entire experience all come together. You can sit back, take it all in, and soak in the moment."
www.foambrewers.com

Burlington is a hub of activity where there's truly something for everyone. Enjoy Lake Champlain from Waterfront Park, stroll along the shore on the Burlington Bike Path, or learn about the lake and its inhabitants at the ECHO Leahy Center for Lake Champlain. If shopping is more your thing, then head to the Church Street Marketplace. At this open air mall you'll also find a wide selection of restaurants and bars; grab a table outside and enjoy some lively street entertainment.

FOLEY BROTHERS BREWING

Brandon

This family-run, seven-barrel brewery offers handcrafted ales and a welcoming tasting room in Brandon, Vermont.

Foley Brothers is best known for its Fair Maiden Double IPA, brewed with seven hop varieties. Part of the Neshobe River Winery, Foley Brothers Brewing products are available in Vermont, Massachusetts, and Connecticut.

FOUR QUARTERS BREWING

Winooski

Specializing in Belgian-style and barrel-aged beers, Four Quarters is a seven-barrel brewery in Winooski's business district.

The lineup in early 2017 included Five Horizons, a five-grain, five-hop IPA; Funky Monkey, a wheat APA with citra; Great Bear, a lightly smoked, chocolate, oatmeal brown ale; and Picklejuice, a fleur–de–lis with hints of honeydew, cucumber, and dill.
www.fourquartersbrewing.com

FROST BEER WORKS

Hinesburg

Owned by Garin and Christina Frost, Frost Beer Works uses high-quality raw materials in their seven-barrel brewery to produce well-balanced flavors. Brewer Mike Lieser makes high-quality products like the Lush Double IPA, the Some Double IPA, the Really Pale Ale, and the Just Pale Ale. Other offerings include Plush, Fall Ale, and the Heavy Imperial Stout. Flavors range from the "seriously" dark, thick beer to light aromatics.

"The types of beer we make are the beers we like to drink: the hoppy, flavorful ales of Vermont," said Frost.
www.frostbeerworks.com

GOOD MEASURE BREWING CO.

Northfield

Good Measure Brewing Co., located in historic downtown Northfield, Vermont, strives to offer its customers beers that range in flavor, texture, and experience. The website claims: "In each of our beers, you'll find something familiar and something distinctly new."

Stop by the tasting room, located at the brewery on East Street, for a sample of the brewery's True Story, brewed with molasses and smoked sea salt; Electric Relaxation, a German-style Berliner-Weisse with kiwi, pineapple, and mango; Wandering Eye, an American rye brown ale; or Firm Hug, the second in their exploration of farmhouse-style hop forward beers.
www.goodmeasurebrewing.com

GOODWATER BREWERY

Williston

Goodwater Brewery's 20bbl brew house and tasting room are located in Williston, offering a modern twist on traditional beer styles. The brewery offers a smooth drinking, full-bodied American pale ale, Hoppy Side of Pale; InspiRED, an Irish red ale that offers an early toffee sweetness; Proper Mild, an English-style ale with a solid malty base; and Sweet Winter Brown, a medium-bodied brown ale with notes of caramel and malt.
www.goodwaterbreweryvt.com

HARPOON BREWERY

Windsor

Harpoon Brewery, founded in 1986, originated in a waterfront warehouse space in Boston. The brewery focuses on quality and "the spirit of fun and enjoyment surrounding our beer and breweries," according to Harpoon's website. The local, state-of-the-art brewing facility is situated in Windsor, Vermont, at the former home of Catamount Brewery.

Harpoon offers a wide variety of products, including ales, stouts, IPAs, hard ciders, and porters. It gained recognition when it introduced Harpoon Winter Warmer, a seasonal craft beer with cinnamon and nutmeg. Other notable beers include Harpoon Octoberfest and Harpoon IPA.
www.harpoonbrewery.com

HERMIT THRUSH BREWERY

Brattleboro

Hermit Thrush combines historical brewing techniques, green tech, and oak casks to offer Belgian-inspired ales. They are proud to employ these processes while minimizing any environmental impact. Located in the heart of downtown Brattleboro, the brewery offers beers with names like Brattlebeer, a sour ale made with locally grown apples; Po Tweet, a pale ale that's available seasonally; Dark at 4:30, a Belgian-style dark ale "to get you through the long nights" with its strong, malty flavor; Dizzy Vicar, a barrel-aged sour dubbel with nots of butterscotch and light caramels; and Tall, Dark & Handsome, a bold, barrel-aged beer with a strong kick.
www.hermitthrushbrewery.com

HILL FARMSTEAD BREWERY

Greensboro

"Shaun Hill started home brewing for a high school science fair project. He got additional experience at various breweries. A common theme in the beers—we want the beers to taste good, and feel good too. We want them soft on the palette," said Phil Young, general manager of Hill Farmstead.

"We always have a very hoppy beer, but we make it so that there are fruity characters without being harsh," Young continued. "We want the beer to be soft and have round edges. We make what we like to drink. We represent our market well.

"Our staple is hoppy for growler fills. We usually have additional pre-packaged bottles as well, with a few barrel-aged offerings and three to four offerings of Farmstead Ales (mixed fermentation with various bacteria. Tart, a little funky.)."

The brewery sits on the land where Shaun Hill's grandfather's dairy barn was located. The barn burned down in 1978. The Hills have been in Greensboro, Vermont, since the 1800s, before there was a town charter.

Today, the brewery is over 9,000 square feet and includes the bottle shop—hoppy beers are purely growlerly fills—and a retail shop. "Our taproom is just across the driveway. There we do growler fills and have six to ten beers on tap," Young commented. "You can taste anything you like on draft. We have a first-class license when we open the tap-room. Now we can serve someone a full beer. We have on-site-only offerings. We do bottle release events; we have been overwhelmed by the support, having lines out the door. We recently did two on-site-only offerings for Double Barrel Damon (imperial stout aged in bourbon bottles, but this was also aged in port barrels), we didn't have too many bottles to sell. We also did Art Plum. If we had offered it as a take-away beer, we would have more people here than bottles to sell," continued Young. "That isn't fun, so we only do the on-site offering."

It has changed a lot in the last five years. At first, it was exclusively "beer-aficionados; people that traveled looking for beer and beer tourism. Now, beer tourism is more mainstream. I used to say that people would come to Vermont to ski, but now visiting breweries is on par with that. We have done tequila/wine/bourbon barrels. The tequila barrel was an experiment, but it was good and we ended up releasing it."

Young explained, "We have several bourbon (some whiskey) barrel aged for porter, stouts, barley barrels." They also use red wine barrels. "The wine brings out the oak character. We use French oak," he noted. "We don't want the wine to shine, we want the beer to come across most. The barrels help with the microoxygenation."

He adds, "We usually let beer sit in barrels for a year to two. Some have gone for almost as long as three years. Barreling is a game of attrition; not all of our bottles end up in the taproom.

"Damon is our most recognizable beer—named for Shaun's black lab who passed away in the early 2000s. Imperial stout aged in bourbon barrels."

Young said, "Shaun's ability is to make beers across so many styles that are the best of their style. A brewery might be known for its IPA, but we do a good job of making great beers in all the styles. The experience of coming to the brewery itself is a special place. The rural setting is a trip. It is an experience. It is not on the way to anywhere. If you're here, you meant to be here."

www.hillfarmstead.com

HOP'N MOOSE BREWING CO.

Rutland

Hop'n Moose is more than a brewery. It's a community gathering place with live music every weekend. Here you can find a selection of eight to twelve ales and lagers and enjoy delicious wood-fired brick oven pizza. Opened in 2014, it was the first brewpub in Rutland.

Options on tap include Lake Monster Lager; Vienna S.M.A.S.H., a single-malt, single-hop, crisp, refreshing lager; Rutland Red, a classic American red ale; Swamp Donkey Stout, an oatmeal stout paired with chocolate and coffee; and Better Dayz, an unfiltered double IPA hopped with citra.

www.hopnmoose.com

House of Fermentology

Burlington

The House of Fermentology is a small beer blender. The beers are fermented and aged slowly in oak barrels. According to the website, they utilize a "mixed culture of saccharomyces and Brettanomyces yeasts along with lactic acid bacteria to make our beers lean, dry, and refreshingly tart. Through our artful blending, this process creates distinctive and original wild ales. All of our beers are alive, unfiltered, and 100 percent bottle conditioned."

Current offerings included two golden ales: Pink Dot, with raspberries, ginger, and lemon zest, and Purple Dot, with blackberries and black currents. The House of Fermentology was also aging Red Dot, a golden wild ale with Balaton and Montmorency tart cherries. *www.houseoffermentology.com*

Idletyme Brewing Co.

Stowe

Idletyme Brewing Co. culminates its values of simplicity, flavorful food, and creativity in all of its products. Idletyme also focuses on food and has a popular restaurant with a ski theme. Its food highlights the bountiful offerings of Vermont, and it emphasizes the importance and value of the farm-to-plate movement.

Idletyme offers lagers, ales, double IPAs, and Belgian-influenced ales on tap at its Mountain Road location in Stowe. Here you can view the state-of-the-art copper brewhouse. *www.idletymebrewing.com*

J'VILLE BREWERY

Jacksonville

J'ville Brewery and its sister company, Honora Winery, are known for small-batch, handcrafted products. The team at J'ville planted Cascade and Newport hops on the vineyard property in 2014, and the brewery received its license in 2015. They specialize in unfiltered ales.

Beers include Saison, aged in Chardonnay barrels from the winery for a hint of chardonnay to the slightly tart beer; Dubbel, a Trappist-style darker beer with hints of dried fruits; Pumpkin Ale, made with minimal spices so the pumpkin flavor shines through; and Vanilla Porter, brewed with Madagascar vanilla bean for a sweet aroma that complements the smooth roasted malt finish. *www.jvillebrewery.com*

KINGDOM BREWING

Newport

"It's a nice place to visit, but a hard place to make a living," said Brian Cook, founder of Kingdom Brewing, in reference to Vermont. "With generations of our family having lived in the Northeast Kingdom, there was no doubt where we wanted to raise our family. But deciding on how to do it is often a long process of trial and error," he continued. "After many years of working in other professions, the Cooks amalgamated their passions of brewing, farming, and building into a successful working family farm and brewery. "We designed and built our tasting room, greenhouse, and operations ourselves to ensure our guests were welcome and enjoyed the freshest and most natural beer in Vermont."

Cook explained how the company started, "My wife and I loved making beer as a hobby, and we were looking for a business that would enable us to stay on the farm. We're able to capitalize on and help build local tourism."

The northernmost brewery in the state, it uses a wood- and propane-fired boiler to heat the wort, and the bedrock is used as an environmentally friendly geothermal-type of fermentation cooling system. "I've got an engineering background, and my wife's background and interest is microbiology, so we were a good fit to design, build, and run the brewery," Cook noted.

The Round Barn Red Ale is their best seller and flagship beverage. "We have some IPAs that people especially enjoy as well. I've got a triple IPA in the tanks right now, 11.5 percent alcohol and something like 119 IBUs. It's balanced, though; we'll package some of it in twenty-two-ounce bottles," Cook said, adding, "My favorite is our Out of Bounds Double IPA."

What's new for 2017 and 2018? "Our growing operation will soon include retail bottle sales. We've added 1,500 feet to the building. There's a clean room, a bottling line, and an expanded tasting room. We'll also have a food cart on-site," Cook said.

"We repurpose a lot of our wood, about 90 percent of wood for the brewery came from other buildings on the property. We try to be very green. We installed Pegas Growler Fillers, which enables us to fill growlers that will keep for a couple of months instead of a few days," he noted.

Cook said that they focus mostly on ales. "And four times a year we use flavorings from the farm to brew beers: Maple Nut Brown Beer, Captain Black's Farmhouse Spruce Saison, Addy Pearl's Maple Dew, and a Pumpkin Doppelbock. For the last beer, we'll freeze the pumpkins, grind them up, and use them in the mash."

As for barrels, Cook said they barrel-age some beers, such as the Russian Imperial Stout, which is aged in Maker's Mark barrels. "We have a grog that's aged in Thomas Tew spiced rum barrels," he added.

Additionally, local ingredients are used whenever possible. "We sugar in the spring but don't use the sap for syrup. We feel we have a better use for it as a natural substitute for water in our recipe. Each year, like the weather, our Maple Nut Brown Beer flavor profile is different but always ends up in the smoothest drinking, most powerful pancake topping you can find," Cook said. "The spent grain is fed to the farm's Angus cattle and the chickens. We also compost the spent hops." *www.kingdombrewingvt.com*

Spanning more than thirty-nine miles, Lake Memphremagog is a glacial lake that links Newport, Vermont, with Magog, Quebec. Stroll along the waterfront and be sure to visit the Northeast Kingdom Tasting Center in the heart of downtown Newport.

Lawson's Finest Liquids

Warren

After twenty-two years of home brewing, Sean Lawson and his wife, Karen, started their award-winning nano brewery. The flagship maple beers and IPAs have an incredible following, both locally and nationally, and Lawson's Finest has received great acclaim at competitions such as the World Beer Cup, Great American Beer Festival, and at two National IPA championships, to name a few.

In 2011, the brewery became so popular that they expanded their facility from a small sugarhouse-style shed into a commercially viable 7bbl system.

Additionally, Lawson now brews a number of his famed IPAs at Two Roads Brewing in Stratford, Connecticut.

Lawson's passion for brewing began when he started home brewing while he was a student at UVM. In 1992, he worked at a few breweries in Colorado and Arizona and then returned to Vermont to develop his fifteen-year career in forestry and environmental education services. All the while, he kept home brewing. Over time, enough people asked Lawson if he could sell them the beer he was making, so he got licensed to become a nano brewer. He described this phase of brewing as a "full-time job with part-time pay." When he bought the seven-barrel system, he was able to finally make the jump to a full-time brewer.

Still passionate about the environment, Lawson continues to lead outings with the naturalist program he founded in 1996 at Mad River Glen ski area. Additionally, Lawson served as president of the Vermont Brewers Association.

Lawson's Sip of Sunshine IPA is the company's flagship product. He says his favorite beer is "the one in my hands right now."

What's new for 2017 and 2018? Lawson's fans can rejoice! They will build a public brewery and taproom that's expected to be completed in the summer of 2018; there are no brewery visits currently. "We will have a brewery and taproom, light food, retail store, admin offices. Also, a year-round beer garden. We are planning on installing a thirty-barrel brewing system," said Lawson. "We will continue to brew at Two Roads (Connecticut) for that local market; [the] Warren, Vermont, brewery will become the pilot facility. The Waitsfield, Vermont, brewery will be for area sales and specialty beer."

Lawson said, "We do new beers every month and cycle through many favorites during the year. I put out two dozen different styles of beer a year." Lawson's maple beers get a lot of well-deserved attention and should be sought out.

Fayston Maple Imperial Stout is brewed with roasted and black malts, almost two gallons of Vermont maple syrup per barrel (thirty-one gallons), and then carefully aged for more than a year in rum barrels from Lawson's friends at Mad River Distillers in Warren, Vermont. This product is among their most sought-after and was made for subzero nights and pairing with decadent desserts.

"When we open up the Waitsfield operation, we will expand the barrel offerings and will include some used barrels to get some funkier beers," Lawson said. "Our beers are fresh and untouched."

Sip of Sunshine and Super Session #2 are run through a centrifuge to remove the yeast and some of the hop particles. "But it's still leaves behind some haziness," Lawson noted.

As for local sourcing, Lawson's uses maple in many beers; and they have a spruce ale and use cedar and balsam tips. "We have access to some local hops. There's a new hop farm in Vermont," Lawson said. "We used them in the Farmhouse IPA, a collaboration beer we did with Two Roads. We included cedar and balsam tips with the hops as well. I also brew a harvest beer once a year with fresh hops I grow at the brewery and at my house."

Like many others in the community, Lawson's offers the spent grain to farmers.

www.lawsonsfinest.com

Long Trail Brewing

Bridgewater Corners

The Long Trail Brewing Company, founded in 1989, takes the term "environmentally conscious" quite seriously. As the website states: "Appreciation for our surroundings and an understanding of the resource limitations of our local environment have inspired our company to consider ways to minimize the environmental impact our brewery has on our area."

The brewery's spent grain and hops become feed for local dairy cattle and serve as a supplement to the nutrient-rich soil. Additionally, they save up to 2,000 gallons of propane a month by using condensed steam from the brewing process and converting it into thermal energy for the brewery. Local ingredients help Long Trail Brewing to achieve their goal of sustainability and environmental consciousness.
www.longtrail.com

Lost Nation Brewing

Morrisville

Allen Van Anda and James Griffith, founders and co-brewmasters of Lost Nation Brewing, spent years learning industry best practices and skills. They created a brewery with the intention and mission of making what they refer to as "honest beer."

The brewery, inspired by European beer styles, is now a 7,000bbl facility. Draughts include Gose, Lost Galaxy, Petit Ardennes, Pitch Black Ale, Rustic Ale, Saison Lamoille, Vermont Pilsner, and Mosaic IPA. Additionally, the taproom serves a menu of local favorites.

The brewing duo share a passion for Vermont life, authentic flavor, modern equipment, and unique beers.
www.lostnationbrewing.com

Madison Brewing Co.

Bennington

The Madison family, with its ties to Bennington, Vermont, purchased a storefront in the town's historic downtown area in the 1990s and turned it into a brewpub. Today, Madison Brewing offers six regular brews as well as a seasonal brew. Famous for Madison's own homemade chips, the brewery is a fun place to enjoy a meal.

Beers include Bennington Blue Blueberry Wheat, brewed with fresh blueberries; Dark Margic, a barrel-aged porter made with maple coffee beans, vanilla beans, and cocoa nibs; Sucker Pond Blonde, a Kölsch-style beer; and Downtown IPA, an American IPA.
www.madisonbrewingco.com

The Molly Stark Scenic Byway connects Bennington and Brattleboro and offers views of Vermont farmland, covered bridges, and the three-state overlook at Hogback Mountain. The path for this route was first carved out in 1777 when General John Stark and his army returned to New Hampshire after the Battle of Bennington.

Magic Hat Brewing Co.

South Burlington

After a long and successful career in and out of the beer industry, Mark Hegedus, who is now general manager at Magic Hat, was brought in when Anheuser-Busch InBev bought Chicago's legendary Goose Island Brewery. Fans of the beer were concerned that the quality of the brews would be compromised after being acquired by the large conglomerate. Hegedus, helped ensure that the quality remained solid as the brew's capacity and distribution expanded. He played a similar role at Magic Hat, after it was bought by another conglomerate, North American Brewers.

While Magic Hat's flagship beverage is obviously #9, Hegedus prefers Belgians, and he says, "My all-time favorite is Rodenbach's Grand Cru. I'm also a big fan of stouts and porters." He adds that someone at Magic Hat "pulled out a bottle of something they called Belgo Sutra, which is quadruple-brewed with figs and dates. Incredible."

What's new for 2017 and 2018? "We're starting a program where we're going to send experimental beers to twenty-five select Vermont craft beer bars to see how people respond. If they like the beers, we may make them commercially. You'll know the beers are on tap in a bar if you see a granite dingbat (part of the Magic Hat logo) tap handle. Additionally, our tasting room is changing. We are adding seating, food, and the ability for customers to order pints. The art space, The Artifactory, will also be expanded," Hegedus detailed.

Magic Hat has a library of more than one hundred beers. Many of them are not known outside of Vermont. Last year, they started bringing some of the favorites back for release, and those are part of the experimental program.

Magic Hat, unlike most breweries, largely uses open fermentation. "It's challenging and iffy, but you can get some great flavors when it's done right," he said. "We also have closed fermenters for the wilder yeasts."

Locally sourced ingredients used include Vermont hops, maple syrup, and local fruit. "It's an important part of who we are," Hegedus said.

Another interesting Magic Hat tradition is Mardi Gras. "Alan Newman, founder of Magic Hat, created Burlington's Mardi Gras celebration. It was about giving back to the community. It's a major fundraiser, and for the last few years [he] has been donating the proceeds to the Vermont Foodbank," Hegedus noted. "We're expanding Mardi Gras into a three- or four-day weekend. We want to attract the best in music and art. Magic Hat has always been about performance, so we're hoping to make Mardi Gras into a destination weekend."

www.magichat.net

McNeill's Brewery

Brattleboro

McNeill's brewery is located in Brattleboro, Vermont. With an impressive twenty-five unique McNeill beers on tap at all times, including Sample Czech and Bavarian Lagers and ales in the styles of Northern Germany, Britain, and the United States, it is certainly worth a visit.

Included in the large variety are six different IPAs, and black and double IPAs. McNeill's Brewery also offers tasty pizzas, Mexican food, and some live music. McNeill's offers something for everyone.

Northshire Brewery

Bennington

Northshire Brewery is a microproducer located in southern Vermont. It offers traditional beer styles including its Equinox Pilsner, Battenkill Ale, Northshire Hefeweizen, Northshire Chocolate Stout, and double IPA Sicilian Pale Ale. Additionally, Northshire offers instructional online videos on home brewing. While in Bennington, visit the historic Bennington Battle Monument, the Bennington Museum, the Silk Road Covered Bridge, and the Burt Henry Covered Bridge.

www.northshirebrewery.com

Norwich Inn

Norwich

Brewmaster Jeremy Hebert creates the well-known, award-winning Jasper Murdock Ales.

According to the Norwich Inn, President James Monroe dined there in 1817, while he was on a lengthy horseback tour of the New England frontier. "Alas, history does not record whether he had a beer, but if he did, it was most likely brewed at the Inn," states the inn's website.

Then, commercial breweries were not in existence in the small state, and local establishments brewed small batches of their own beers for guests. The website states, "Even the largest still at the time was only large enough for what the brewer and his guests could enjoy. This brewing tradition was

reinstated at the Inn in 1993, when Jasper Murdock's Alehouse looked to the well-loved history (or fable as the case may be) and began producing English-style traditional ales."
www.norwichinn.com/brewery

OTTER CREEK BREWING CO.

Middlebury

Otter Creek Brewing, which creates hop-soaked ales and lagers, "has been hitting, hopping, and dosing brews with creativity since acid-wash jeans were hip," according to their website.

In 2016, they added a 120-barrel brew house and a 9,000-square-foot addition to their location on Exchange Street in Middlebury.

At OCB there's a focus on sustainability, with spent grains feeding local dairy cows and spent hops and yeast donated to farmers as an alternative fertilizer. In addition, OCB is working with the Non-GMO Project to validate their ingredients.

Brews available year-round include Backseat Berner, Couch Surfer, Steampipe, and Daily Dose IPA. Seaonal offerings include Citra Mantra IPL, Fresh Slice, and Overgrown APA. Also offered seasonally is Orange Dream Cream Ale.

For 2017, the website states that they plan to continue the "cosmic journey" with "the creations of some killer new recipes, letting our collective freak flags fly whenever possible."
www.ottercreekbrewing.com

PROHIBITION PIG

Waterbury

Well loved by locals and tourists alike, Prohibition Pig offers classic cocktails, craft beer, and barbecue. If the constant line at the restaurant gives any indication of its flavors, then these are top-notch.

Prohibition Pig's offering on the draft menu includes Bantam Double IPA; Little Fluffy Clouds, brewed with two types of pale malt and flaked oats; Swine Cooler, made with raspberries and sour cherries; Slushie Snow Lager, brewed with Amarillo and Nelson hops; and Make Em Say Goes-uhhh, a gose-style, kettle-soured beer.
www.prohibitionpig.com

Queen City Brewery

Burlington

"I went to school for chemistry and started home brewing after grad school in 1986. In 2012, I wrote the business plan, and some friends and family went in with me on it," said Paul Hale, founder of Queen City Brewery.

Hale founded Queen City Brewery in 2012 with several partners: Paul Held, Phil Kaszuba, Maarten van Ryckevorsel, and Sarah van Ryckevorsel. The actual brewery, located in a renovated warehouse in Burlington, opened in 2014. Hale, who is now managing partner and brewmaster, had an idea for a tasting room, but that idea changed after he scored a large mahogany bar from a private club that had closed. The larger bar meant he needed a larger space, which meant a different license, which meant he needed to serve food.

The tasting room offers many of the brewery's beers at the bar and serves sparkling hard cider from a local cidery, Citizen Cider, along with wines. They even serve root beer from a Burlington soda producer, but no hard liquor.

Queen City's bestselling beer and flagship beverage is the Yorkshire Porter. "We also sell a lot of our South End Lager, a helles style. [It] does really well in the greater Boston area, and in the summer our Hefeweizen is popular," Hale said.

What's new for 2017 and 2018? "Last year we started a barrel-aging program called 'Pint Street' Barrel Aged Series. The beers are mostly strong styles, but also regular strength, such as a saison. We'll be doing more of that," Hale noted. "We're using chardonnay and cab franc barrels from a winery on Long Island. We're bottling the batches. We're also getting a twelve-ounce bottling line installed. Should be ready in a month or so."

Customers describe Queen City as "traditional and authentic," which is ironic now, since most breweries are going with hop-heavy IPAs using American hops. "We do have one IPA that uses traditional English hops," said Hale. "All our beers are brewed with the traditional malt, hops, and yeast for that style and for that country. We even adjust the water chemistry to mimic the city that the beer comes from. Our water in Burlington is quite soft, so we can easily add the right kind of salts. Since we focus on traditional styles, all of our beers would also be described as approachable and food-friendly."

Queen City focuses on traditional European-style ales and lagers, such as Landlady ESB, Yorkshire Porter, City Beer, South End Lager, Hefeweizen, Munich Dunkel, Steinbier, Rauchbier (they smoke their own malt), Oktoberfest, Maibock, Gregarious Scotch Ale, and Barge Canal Oatmeal Stout.

As of now they don't have a sour program, but "there are some naturally occurring Brettanomyces in the wine barrels, which gives the aged beers a secondary fermentation. But it's not like a lactic acid sour," said Hale.

"We have recently introduced our 'Pint Street' Barrel Aged Series here at the brewery," Hale added. Available in 500ml bottles is Old Monty Barleywine-Style Ale aged in Chardonnay barrels and Lillian's Saison, which is aged for six months in Cabernet Franc barrels with indigenous Brettanomyces.

Lagering happens for four or five weeks. All of Queen City's fermentation is done in individually temperature-controlled glycol-jacketed tanks so they can do lagering.

Nothing is sourced locally, and that disappoints some people. "Because we're brewing traditional European beers we source all our ingredients from those countries," Hale explained. "Right now, in the bar we have fourteen beers on tap in the bar; you can only maintain so many styles. Plus, we have seasonal beers to brew. We do a bock in the spring and an Oktoberfest in the fall.

Queen City Brewer's Assistant Brewer, Ben Gostanian, was previously an assistant brewer and jack-of-all-trades at Farnham Brewery.

We do an occasional Rauchbier. We smoke our own malt in the parking lot for Rauchbier."

The spent grain is used by beef farmers who come and pick it up. "They claim the cows come running toward the truck. The cows really like it. Many of the farmers work in town, so I can call them and then they come in to pick it up after their day job," Hale said.

"We brew a unique style beer in the fall called Steinbier, or stone beer. I don't think there are any breweries doing it regularly anymore. I did it as a home brewer for twenty years in my backyard. We build a beechwood fire in the parking lot and heat 300 pounds of rocks until they are about 1,200 degrees, and we lower the rocks into the brewing kettle. The hot rocks caramelize the malt sugars, give it a touch of smoke, and a touch of mineral," Hale described. "It's ready by Christmastime. The idea came from the Michael Jackson TV program called the *Beer Hunter*. We make an event out of it. Takes about ten batches of rocks to make the beer. I'm doing this kind of for fun, but I have to say, one of the most rewarding things has been creating local jobs. We now have three full-time employees."

www.queencitybrewery.net

RED BARN BREWING

Danville

Red Barn Brewing, located in an 1840s barn, is a nano brewery creating and serving small batches of finely crafted beer. Offerings include Porters, English, Kölsch, Wheat, Lagers, APAs, and IPAs. The creative names say quite a bit about the fun-loving spirit of the producers, and Red Barn makes everything from the Evil Angle to the Whiplash Wheat to the Little Devil.

Styles range from classic German Kölsch to refreshing Bavarian wheat beers and hoppy IPAs. For single-barrel lovers, they also make their beloved "Lithium," which is a single-hop series of DIPA.
www.redbarnbrewingvt.com

If you find yourself in Danville in the fall, then a stop at the Great Vermont Corn Maze is a must. For those daring enough, Dead North, a haunted corn maze experience like no other, is worth the price of admission.

RIVER ROOST BREWERY

White River Junction

Located in the downtown area of White River Junction, River Roost Brewery is a staple on the microbeer scene. With a 4.25 out of a possible 5 from the *Beer Advocate*, and a production of more than seventeen beers, this is an interesting spot.
www.riverroostbrewery.com

ROCK ART BREWERY

Morrisville

Located north of Stowe, in the village of Morrisville, Vermont, Rock Art Brewery is known for its growlers, kegs, and art. The Rock Art facility offers a viewing area where visitors can watch the production process of beers like their Ridge Runner, Whitetail, American Red, IPA, Midnight Madness, and Riddler, to name a few. The eclectic retail shop carries a variety of Vermont foods, works by unique Vermont artists, and fun Rock Art swag. Other points of interest in the area: the Morrisville Historical Society and the Greek Revival buildings of the town.
www.rockartbrewery.com

Saint J Brewery

Saint Johnsbury Center

Saint J brews are American Blonde, Belgian Strong Dark, and Smokin' J IPA. The brewery also offers food and a bar that's decorated for owner Scott Salmonsen's favorite baseball team: the Boston Red Sox. Other points of interest in the area include the slopes at Burke Mountain, the Kingdom Trails, Maplewood Lodge, and Juniper's Restaurant at The Wildflower Inn.

www.saintjbrewery.com

Simple Roots Brewing

Burlington

Founded by Dan Ukolowicz and Kara Pawlusiak, a husband-and-wife team, Simple Roots is now in its third year of production. Located in Burlington, Simple Roots is part of an active local brewery culture and is worth a visit on your stops to see others in town. Its simple philosophy embodies the art of easy living, like lawn games and BBQs and, of course, beer. Simple Roots, as they state on their website, is "all about life's simple pleasures like beer, friends, and family," and this is emphasized by its customer-friendly clean growler program. Simple Roots will fill absolutely any clean growler, which is a great environmentally conscious practice.

www.simplerootsbrewing.com

Stone Corral Brewery

Richmond

Adjacent to the taproom, the Stone Corral Brewery offers more than a dozen selections, and visitors can enjoy a viewing of the beer-making process. Food and regular live music make this a welcome spot. Beers include the infamous Wiley's Expedition with its crisp, hoppy flavor. The website says that this extra pale ale "is packed with Citra, Meridian, and Amarillo hops. Celebrating life's expeditions, large and small." The Raspberry Black, another of their flagship beers, is noted to include an infusion of "raspberries and French Oak. Layers of malt and mocha are highlighted with berry aroma and a note of vanilla."

www.stonecorral.com

Switchback Brewing Co.

Burlington

Burlington's South End is home to this brewery that has been open since 2002. The taproom showcases their bottling line and a variety of beers that are always on tap: the flagship Switchback Ale, an unfiltered, reddish-amber ale made using only traditional ingredients; Connector IPA, designed to showcase the citrus, tropical fruit, and pine characteristics of the hops; and select rotating specials, such as Slow-Fermented Brown Ale and Dooley's Belated Porter.

www.switchbackvt.com

Ten Bends Beer

Hyde Park

Mike Scarlata and Jason Powell, co-owners of Ten Bends Beer, began brewing in a "deep" north woods Vermont shed, where they experimented with production of all-grain beers. Although their first machinery was a converted 1960s stainless steel coffee maker, the brewery now produces some of Vermont's beloved beer.

Located in a 1,400-square-foot facility, Ten Bends creates small-batch ales with a focus on resources from their beloved Vermont. The brewery has an open-air tasting room with a scenic view that guests enjoy while imbibing signature beers like the Cold Moon Black Ale, the Ava Amber, and the Evolution Series DIPAs.

www.tenbendsbeer.com

The Alchemist

Waterbury

In 1994, John Kimmich came to Vermont with the express purpose of studying the craft of brewing from industry leader, and now friend, Greg Noonan. Kimmich got his industry stripes working as Head Brewer at Vermont Pub and Brewery in Burlington, Vermont, where he met Jen. With their combined knowledge and experience, the couple opened The Alchemist. The brewery rapidly developed a cult following and garnered national and international acclaim in the beer circuit.

John and Jen Kimmich originally opened The Alchemist as a sixty-seat brewpub in the village of Waterbury in 2003. After eight years of success and growing popularity, they decided to open a small production brewery. Today, The Alchemist currently operates two breweries in Vermont and handles all local distribution. It is one of the top-rated beer companies in America.

The Kimmiches have quite a large following and are constantly inundated with requests for Heady Topper, which has been rated as high as "No. 1 beer in the world" on sites like *Beer Advocate*.

The Alchemist can't keep up with demand, despite the fact that they brew 2,000 cases of the hop-drenched beverage a week, distributing it to retailers around Waterbury. Typically, it sells out the day it hits the shelf, and the lines at the brewery are something to see.

Both Heady Topper and Focal Banger were voted two of the world's best in 2016, so the Alchemist really is home to two flagship beverages.

As of December 2015, Heady Topper was rated the fifth best beer in the world by *Beer Advocate* and has been described as "a complex web of genius." It is not unusual for fans to travel long distances to try and purchase the beer from retail stores in Vermont. Most retailers have a limit of two four-packs per customer, including the brewery itself, which can create quite a buying frenzy on release days.

The brewery in Stowe produces about 180 barrels of beer per week, or roughly 9,000 barrels per year. "When we talk about expansion, we're always talking in terms of our local market and our own visitors' center," Kimmich said. "We're looking at little bumps [in production] so that we can really service our community and the people that come to our brewery."

Jen Kimmich added, "Our hope is that the beer tourists will come to us and buy as much as they can, while the locals will still be able to buy what they need. There are plenty of breweries our size that are selling everything out their door. We know we can do that, too, but it seems shortsighted. We've come to terms with the fact that we're not going to make everyone happy, but we do our best."
www.alchemistbeer.com

TROUT RIVER BREWING CO.

Springfield

Located in Springfield, Vermont, Trout River was founded by Dan and Laura Gates in 1996. Current owners Kelen Beardsley, Gabriel Streeter, and Trevor Billings are incorporated under Vermont Beer Shapers, LTD. "We want to keep the traditions and some of the great beers Dan has created over the

years, while making Trout River our own," said Beardsley, president of Trout River.

They make a Rainbow Red, Vermont Single IPA, Arbor Knot Double IPA, Hefewummps, Hangry Angler, and a Chocolate Oatmeal Stout.

Other points of interest in Springfield include the historic Eureka Schoolhouse, built in 1790, the Hartness Mansion, and Tory's Cave.
www.troutriverbrewing.com

VERMONT PUB & BREWERY

Burlington

In 1986, a man by the name of Greg Noonan published a book that would change the beer industry forever. That book was called *Brewing Lager Beer* and became an industry bible.

The famed Greg Noonan opened the Vermont Pub & Brewery in 1988, and it has the esteemed title of being the state's original brewpub, and longest running craft brewery, which in a state chock-full of breweries is quite a claim to fame.

Noonan's expertise has informed the practices of many Vermont breweries, but his start was anything but easy: "I had $175,000, which is a shoestring budget in the brewing industry; brewing equipment is very expensive," says the website. Noonan "applied to several banks for additional funds, but lenders were skeptical. The banks all said,

'What is a brewpub?' But I plunged on anyway with the money I had."

Noonan's book, *Brewing Lager Beer: The Most Comprehensive Book for Home- and Microbreweries*, is considered by many to be the gold standard of beer insight. "You're not going to find a successful brewer in the country that doesn't have a dog-eared copy of this book," says John Kimmich, Noonan's protégé and co-owner of The Alchemist Pub & Brewery in Waterbury. "It is the definitive book on brewing lager beer."

Their award-winning beers are unpasteurized and unfiltered. www.vermontbrewery.com

von Trapp Brewery

Stowe

The von Trapp Brewery, opened in the spring of 2010, was more than a decade in the making. Founded by Johannes von Trapp, of the famed singing family, the brewery is on the family's majestic property that is home to the beloved von Trapp Family Lodge.

Von Trapp's love of his native Austrian countryside lagers inspired the brewery's offerings, and Johannes and his son, Sam, have worked diligently to bring these traditional flavors to Vermont.

The duo purchased state-of-the-art equipment and seemingly spared no expense to bring the finest quality product to market. The brewery now produces 50,000 gallons of lager each year in its 30,000-square-foot facility.

Brewmaster JP Williams has brewed for von Trapp Brewing since 2012. Williams cut his teeth in the industry brewing for Magic Hat and working as their general manager before he came to von Trapp Brewing.

"My quality of life is up tenfold, the people are outstanding, and the scenic views are breathtaking," said Williams about moving to the countryside and working for the notable family. "Waking up every day and seeing the Worcester Range while brewing the state's best lagers is just heaven."

von Trapp uses all German malts and hops including a malt from the Czech Republic.

As for the flagship beverage, Sam von Trapp said, "it is the Helles. It was the first one we brewed. The pilsner has picked up a lot of steam after winning awards."

von Trapp's personal favorites are also the Helles. "I like the low alcohol aspect," he noted. "We've also been creating a few specialty brews, sometimes incorporating local ingredients. It's fun and gives the brewers more chance for creative expression. These are available on-site."

What's new for 2017 and 2018? "We will be brewing a Kölsch-style beer, which is new for us. We will also be brewing a double-IPL (India Pale Lager)," von Trapp continued. "These will both have some limited local distribution, but we always try to have some of the specialty beers on-site for guests."

As for a barrel program, von Trapp added, "We took some of our Trösten Lager, which is a dark winter seasonal beer, and aged it in Jack Daniel's barrels for eleven months. It was available only in Vermont."

He continued, "The Helles is the only filtered beer we have, and none of them are pasteurized. I think it makes for a healthier beer. It was an early decision by my father to brew using traditional methods. My father found an artesian spring using old maps. He bought the property and used the water for the lodge. He later found that it had the perfect mineral profile for brewing lagers."

The spent grain is fed to their cattle. "Because we are using spent grain, it has none of the negative health impacts of unfermented grain. And the cattle love it. We use a tractor to pull a trailer that spreads the grain out for the cattle. They can tell by the sound of the tractor that the grain is coming and they follow along. Feeding the grain to the cattle also helps to bring additional nutrition back into the land," von Trapp explained.

"One of the keys to making our beers is the ROLEC brew house from Bavaria. In addition to giving us precise temperature controls, we can naturally carbonate the beer, which protects the flavors," he said.

In addition, he noted, "We recently completed a collaboration beer with a Bavarian brewery. It was a hoppy Märzen-style lager. We hope to do more collaborations in the future."

In conclusion, von Trapp said, "There's a lot of outdoor recreation here. In the winter, it's quite common to see people cross-country skiing; they can glide right up to the Bierhall and brewery."
www.vontrappbrewing.com

WHETSTONE STATION

Brattleboro

The Whetstone Station Restaurant and Brewery offers regional micro-brewed and international beers served with a menu that emphasizes comfort food, small plates, and items from the grill. It sources local products whenever possible and has a pleasant fire-lit dining room and outdoor deck adjacent to a rooftop biergarten that overlooks the Connecticut River and Mount Wantastiquet. Here they brew only six kegs of beer a year and consider themselves to be "experimental." An additional point of interest is the Vermont-New Hampshire state line that actually runs right through their tasting room and is painted on the floor.

They make an IPA, a Hoppy Amber, and a Pilsner.
www.whetstonestation.com

Zero Gravity Craft Brewery

Burlington

Zero Gravity produces classic beers from the best malt and hops possible. Their focus is on quality, technique, and recipes. Brewmaster Paul Sayler, Head of Production Justin McCarthy, and Flatbread Head Brewer Destiny Saxon are committed to all aspects of the brewing process.

Famously recognized for its pizza, the brewery is part of the organic wood-fired pizza company, American Flatbread. The second location is home to a beer garden with views to the canning operation and retail shop and is located in Burlington's exciting Pine Street district. Beers include a Pilsner, an English Brown Ale, and a Belgian Triple.
www.zerogravitybeer.com

DRINK VERMONT
COCKTAIL RECIPES

Inspired by the rich and varied flavors of Vermont, famed mixologists Andie Ferman and Darren Crawford created cocktail recipes to showcase the palates of the distilleries and cideries, wineries, and breweries represented in the Green Mountain State.

THE RED CLOVER CLUB

A riff on the Traditional Clover Club

Ingredients:
¼ ounce Red Bean Aquafaba
½ ounce Raspberry Liqueur
1½ ounces Terroir Gin
¾ ounce Lemon Juice
Ice
Sage Leaf

Directions:
Dry shake the Red Bean Aquafaba in a shaker, then add the raspberry liqueur, gin, lemon juice, and ice in a shaker and shake.

Pour into a glass, garnish with a sage leaf, and serve.

Mixed by Andie Ferman

THE HONEY BEE PLEASE

A riff on the Bee's Knees

Ingredients:
   1½ ounces Botanivore Gin
   ¾ ounce Lemon Juice
   ½ ounce Honey Simple Syrup
   Spritz of Absinthe
   Ice
   Lemon Twist

Directions:
Combine the gin, lemon juice, honey simple syrup, absinthe, and ice in a shaker and shake.

Pour into a glass, garnish with a lemon twist, and serve.

Mixed by Andie Ferman

DRY RYE AMERICAN PIE

Ingredients:
1½ ounces Dry Rye Gin
½ ounce Maple Syrup
¾ ounce Apple Juice
¼ ounce Lemon Juice
2 dashes of Baked Apple Bitters
Ice
Cinnamon Stick
Apple Slice
Ground Cinnamon

Directions:
Combine the gin, maple syrup, apple juice, lemon juice, Baked Apple Bitters, and ice in a shaker and shake!

Pour into a glass, garnish with a cinnamon stick and apple slice dusted with cinnamon, then serve.

Mixed by Andie Ferman

THESE GREEN MOUNTAINS

Ingredients:
½ ounce Green Chartreuse
1½ ounces Terroir Gin
¾ ounce Lime Juice
¼ ounce Maple Syrup
Ice
Rosemary Sprig

Directions:
Combine the green chartreuse, gin, lime juice, maple syrup, and ice in a shaker and shake.

Pour into a glass, garnish with a rosemary sprig, and serve.

Mixed by Andie Ferman

MILKY WAY BACK

Ingredients:
2 ounces Rye Whiskey
½ ounce Chai Tea Concentrate
1 ounce Almond Milk
¼ ounce Cherry Syrup
Cherry

Directions:
Combine the whiskey, chai tea concentrate, almond milk, and cherry syrup in a shaker and shake.

Pour into a milk jug, garnish with a cherry, and serve.

Mixed by Andie Ferman

You Think That's Funny Meow?

Ingredients:
½ ounce Banana Liqueur
1½ ounces Green Chile Vodka
½ ounce Lime Juice
Barspoon of Bruto Americano
Ice
Lime Wheel

Directions:
Combine the banana liqueur, green chile vodka, lime juice, Bruto Americano, and ice in a shaker and shake.

Pour into a glass, garnish with a lime wheel, and serve.

Mixed by Andie Ferman

Autumn Splendor

Ingredients:
  ½ ounce Spiced Pear Liqueur
  1½ ounces All-Purpose Vodka
  ½ ounce Apple Juice
  ½ ounce Lemon Juice
  Ice
  Cinnamon

Directions:
Combine the pear liqueur, vodka, apple juice, lemon juice, and ice in a shaker and shake.

Pour into a glass, garnish with a dusting of cinnamon, and serve.

Mixed by Andie Ferman

Madame Maple

Ingredients:
½ ounce Maple Syrup
1 ounce Pear Brandy
½ ounce Rye Whiskey
Ice
Maple Candy

Directions:
Combine the maple syrup, brandy, whiskey, and ice in a shaker and shake.

Pour into a glass, garnish with a piece of maple candy, and serve.

Mixed by Andie Ferman

Monarch Butter-Rye

Ingredients:
½ ounce Hot Butter
1½ ounces Dry Rye Reposado
¾ ounce Spiced Pear Liqueur
½ ounce Lemon Juice
Cinnamon Stick

Directions:
Heat butter, then combine the reposado, pear liqueur, and lemon juice in heat-safe glass and stir.

Garnish with a cinnamon stick. Serve hot!

Mixed by Andie Ferman

FREEDOM AND UNITY!

Ingredients:
½ ounce Cali Citrus Vodka
1 ounce Vermont White Vodka
¼ ounce Lillet
Ice
Lemon and Orange Peels

Directions:
Combine the vodkas, Lillet, and ice in a glass and stir.

Pour into a glass and garnish with lemon and orange peels intertwined.

Mixed by Andie Ferman

HERMIT BLUSH

Ingredients:
1½ ounces Cali Citrus Vodka
½ ounce Lime Juice
½ ounce Raspberry Liqueur
Ice

Directions:
Combine the vodka, lime juice, raspberry liqueur, and ice in a shaker and shake!

Pour into a glass and serve.

Mixed by Andie Ferman

AMERICANO SPRITZ

Ingredients:
    1½ ounces Cali Citrus Vodka
    ½ ounce Bruto Americano
    Ice
    Soda Water
    Cinnamon Stick
    Ginger Slice

Directions:
Combine the vodka, Bruto, and ice in a glass, then top with soda water.

Garnish with a cinnamon stick and ginger slice and serve.

Mixed by Andie Ferman

Rye Oh Rye

Ingredients:
   2 ounces Rye Whiskey
   ½ ounce Aperol
   Ice
   Grapefruit Peel

Directions:
Combine the whiskey, Aperol, and ice in a shaker and shake.

Pour into a glass, garnish with grapefruit peel, and serve.

Mixed by Andie Ferman

Snow on the Rock

Ingredients:
   Salt
   Pepper
   Chili Powder
   1½ ounces Vermont White Vodka
   ¾ ounce Lillet
   ¼ ounce Dolin Dry Vermouth
   Ice Cube

Directions:
Combine the salt, pepper, and chili powder. Rim a glass with the mixture and set aside.

Combine the vodka, Lillet, vermouth, and ice in a shaker and shake.

Pour into the rimmed glass and serve.

Mixed by Andie Ferman

SPICED GREEN MOUNTAIN

Ingredients:
1½ ounces Spiced Pear Liqueur
¼ ounce Absinthe
Soda Water

Directions:
Build in glass and top with soda water.

Mixed by Andie Ferman

WHISKEY SUNSET

Ingredients:
½ ounce Raspberry Liqueur
1½ ounces Rye Whiskey

Directions:
Layer in a glass, pouring in the denser raspberry liqueur first, and then pouring the whiskey over a bar spoon.

Mixed by Andie Ferman

ICE ON THE LAKE

Ingredients:
½ ounce Aquafaba
½ ounce Raspberry Liqueur
1½ ounces Foam-Rye Whiskey

Directions:
Shake the Aquafaba and then pour with raspberry liqueur and whiskey.

Mixed by Andie Ferman

An Icey Glimpse

Ingredients:
Ice Sphere
¾ ounce Raspberry Liqueur
1 ounce Absinthe
Water

Directions:
Place ice sphere in glass. Pour in the raspberry liqueur and then the absinthe. Top with water.

Mixed by Andie Ferman

FREAKY TIKI PEAR

Ingredients:
1½ ounces Pear EDV
1 ounce Spiced Pear Liqueur
½ ounce Lime Juice
¼ ounce Orange Juice
Crushed Ice
Lime Slice
Slice of Fresh Ginger
Angostura Bitters

Directions:
Combine the pear EDV, pear liqueur, lime juice, and orange juice in a shaker and shake.

Pour into a glass over crushed ice. Garnish with a lime slice, ginger, and bitters.

Mixed by Andie Ferman

THE RYES AND SHINE

Ingredients:
2 ounces Rye Whiskey
¾ ounce Orange Juice
¼ ounce Grenadine
Ice

Directions:
Combine all ingredients together with ice in a shaker and shake.

Pour into a glass and serve.

Mixed by Andie Ferman

AMORE

Ingredients:
1 ounce Amaro Nonino
¾ ounce Silo Cacao Vodka
¾ ounce Lemon Juice
¼ ounce Maple Syrup
½ ounce Egg Whites
2 dashes Old Fashioned Bitters
Angostura Bitters

Directions:
Combine the Amaro Nonino, vodka, lemon juice, maple, syrup, and egg whites in a tin. Shake vigorously for fifteen seconds.

Strain into a couple glass and garnish with bitters.

Mixed by Darren Crawford

ALPINE ASCENSION

Ingredients:
Fresh Rosemary
¾ ounce Lemon Juice
1½ ounces Dolin Blanc
1 ounce Campari
½ ounce Maple Syrup
Lemon Slice
Fresh Cracked Black Peppercorns

Directions:
Muddle some rosemary in a mixing tin with the lemon juice.

Add the Dolin Blanc, Campari, and maple syrup and shake, then double strain into a tumbler.

Garnish with a rosemary sprig, lemon slice, and freshly ground black peppercorns.

Mixed by Darren Crawford

AGENT SMITH

Ingredients:
1½ ounces Mad River Revolution Rye
½ ounce Punt e Mes
½ ounce Green Chartreuse
¼ ounce Maraschino Liqueur
2 dashes Xocolatl Mole Bitters
Orange Peel

Directions:
Add the rye, Punt e Mes, chartreuse, maraschino liqueur, and bitters to a mixing glass, stir to dilution, then strain into a small cocktail glass.

Garnish with the oil from an orange peel.

Mixed by Darren Crawford

GREEN MOUNTAIN

Ingredients:
¾ ounce Green Mountain Gin
¾ ounce Silo Cucumber Vodka
½ ounce Green Chartreuse
¾ ounce Lime Juice
½ ounce Pineapple Syrup
3 dashes Absinthe
Cucumber Ribbon
Edible Flowers

Directions:
Shake the gin, vodka, chartreuse, lime juice, pineapple syrup, and absinthe, then fine strain into a coupe or martini glass.

Garnish with a long ribbon of cucumber and edible flowers.

Mixed by Darren Crawford

Tapping the Admiral

Ingredients:

2 ounces Mad River Vanilla Rum
½ ounce Velvet Falernum
½ ounce Coconut Ginger Syrup
½ ounce Lime Juice
3 dashes Old Fashioned Bitters
Pebble Ice
Fresh Ginger
Lime Wedge

Directions:

Add the rum, Velvet Falernum, coconut ginger syrup, lime juice, and bitters to a mixing tin with pebble ice. Shake quickly for two seconds, then pour into a tumbler.

Garnish with fresh ginger and lime.

Mixed by Darren Crawford

BRAMBLIN MAN

Ingredients:

1½ ounces Barr Hill Gin
1 ounce Lemon Juice
½ ounce Raspberry-Rhubarb Syrup
1½ ounces Boyden Rhubarb Wine
Pebble Ice
¼ ounce Boyden Cassis
Mint Sprigs
Lemon Zest

Directions:

Add the gin, lemon juice, raspberry-rhubarb syrup, and rhubarb wine to a collins glass. Add pebble ice and stir well.

Float the cassis on top, then garnish with mint sprigs and lemon zest.

Mixed by Darren Crawford

DANDY SHANDY

Ingredients:
1½ ounces Smugglers' Notch Litigation Wheat Whiskey
¾ ounce Lemon Juice
½ ounce Unfiltered Apple Juice
½ ounce Honey Syrup
Large Ice Cube
1 ounce Flag Hill Farm Vermont Cider
Pear Slice
Fresh Cinnamon

Directions:
Shake together the whiskey, lemon juice, apple juice, and honey syrup, then strain into a stemmed beer glass with a large cube of ice.

Float the cider on top and garnish with a slice of pear and fresh cinnamon.

Mixed by Darren Crawford

PAPILIO SOUR

Ingredients:
3 Kumquats
1 ounce Appalachian Papilio
1 ounce Cointreau
1 ounce Cocchi Americano
1 ounce Lemon Juice
Mint Leaf

Directions:
Muddle two of the kumquats in a mixing tin. Add the Appalachian Papilio, Cointreau, Cocchi Americano, and lemon juice. Shake well, then fine strain into a coupe glass.

Garnish with the remaining kumquat and a mint leaf.

Mixed by Darren Crawford

Vermont Smash

Ingredients:
Mint Leaves
Lemon Wedge
Whole Strawberry
2 ounces Appalachian Snowfall Whiskey
$\frac{1}{4}$ ounce Maple Syrup
Pebble Ice
Mint Sprig
Strawberry Slices

Directions:
Muddle some mint leaves, a lemon wedge, and a strawberry in a julep cup.

Add the whiskey and maple syrup and stir well with pebble ice.

Garnish with a mint sprig and strawberry slices.

Mixed by Darren Crawford

LATE BREAKFAST

Ingredients:
1½ ounces Mad River Revolution Rye
½ ounce Appalachian Kaffevan Coffee Liqueur
¼ ounce Saxton's Sapling Maple Liqueur
2 dashes Orange Bitters
Large Ice Cube
3 Coffee Beans
Orange Twist

Directions:
Stir together the rye, coffee liqueur, maple liqueur, and bitters in a mixing glass to dilution.

Pour into a tumbler with a large cube of ice.

Garnish with coffee beans and an orange twist.

Mixed by Darren Crawford

Maple Sage Fizz

Ingredients:
4 to 5 Fresh Sage Leaves
¾ ounce Lemon Juice
2 ounces Dunc's Mill Maple Rum
½ ounce Maple Syrup
½ ounce Egg Whites
2 dashes Angostura Bitters
Ice
1 ounce Seltzer
Fresh Grated Nutmeg

Directions:
Muddle three to four sage leaves with the lemon juice in a mixing tin.

Add the rum, maple syrup, egg whites, and bitters, then shake for five seconds.

Add ice and shake for fifteen seconds, then strain into a small fizz glass without the ice.

Top with seltzer. Garnish with the remaining sage leaf and nutmeg.

Mixed by Darren Crawford

POLLENATOR

Ingredients:
1½ ounces Silo Lavender Vodka
½ ounce Cognac
¾ ounce Lemon Juice
½ ounce Honey Syrup
Lemon Wheel
Fresh Lavender Petals

Directions:
Shake together the vodka, cognac, lemon juice, and honey syrup, then strain it into a coupe or martini glass.

Garnish with a lemon wheel and fresh lavender petals.

Mixed by Darren Crawford

ALL HOPPED UP

Ingredients:
1½ ounces Smugglers' Notch Gin
½ ounce Cointreau
½ ounce Boyden Gold Leaf Wine
1 dash Orange Bitters
Lemon Peel

Directions:
Stir the gin, Cointreau, wine, and bitters to dilution, then strain into a small cocktail glass.

Garnish with the oil from a lemon peel.

Mixed by Darren Crawford

DEVIL'S KISS

Ingredients:
1½ ounces Stonecutter Single Barrel Gin
½ ounce St. George Raspberry Liqueur
½ ounce Cocchi Americano Rosa
2 dashes Peychaud's Bitters
2 dashes Absinthe
Strawberry or Raspberry

Directions:
Stir the gin, raspberry liqueur, Americano Rosa, bitters, and absinthe to dilution in a mixing glass, then strain into a small cocktail glass.

Garnish with a fresh berry and serve.

Mixed by Darren Crawford

Lion's Share

Ingredients:
1½ ounces Saxton's Sapling Maple Bourbon
½ ounce Manzanilla Sherry
½ ounce Orange Syrup
½ ounce Vanilla Syrup
¾ ounce Lemon Juice
2 dashes Angostura Bitters
1 ounce Ginger Beer
Rocks
Lemon Wedge
Mint Sprig
Fresh Grated Nutmeg

Directions:
Add the bourbon, sherry, orange syrup, vanilla syrup, lemon juice, and bitters to a mixing tin and shake well. Strain into a collins glass and top with ginger beer.

Garnish with a lemon wedge, mint sprig, and fresh grated nutmeg.

Mixed by Darren Crawford

SWEETWATER SPRITZ

Ingredients:
2 Grapefruit Slices
2 Lemon Slices
2 Lime Slices
1 Strawberry, Sliced
1 ounce Aperol
1½ ounces Vermont Ice Hard Cider
2 ounces Sweetwater Maple Seltzer

Directions:
Garnish the inside of a wine glass with the fresh citrus and strawberry slices.

Add ice and remaining ingredients.

Mixed by Darren Crawford

Monarchy

Ingredients:

1½ ounces Papilio
¾ ounce Pamplemousse
½ ounce Carpano Bianco
½ ounce Lime Juice
Big Ice Cube
1½ ounces Fever Tree Mediterranean Tonic
Grapefruit Slice
Lime Slice
Fresh Rosemary Sprig

Directions:

Add the first four ingredients to a mixing tin, shake well, then fine strain into a tumbler over a big ice cube.

Add the Fever Tree Mediterranean Tonic, grapefruit and lime slices, and a sprig of fresh rosemary.

Mixed by Darren Crawford

THE CHAPMAN

Ingredients:
1 ounce Vermont Spirits Crimson Vodka
¾ ounce No. 14 Apple Brandy
¾ ounce St. George Pear Liqueur
2 dashes Cinnamon Tincture
Apple Slice
Fresh Grated Cinnamon

Directions:
Stir the vodka, apple brandy, pear liqueur, and cinnamon tincture to dilution in a mixing glass.

Strain into a small cocktail glass and garnish with an apple slice and fresh grated cinnamon.

Mixed by Darren Crawford

MAD RIVER TEA PARTY

Ingredients:
2 ounces Mad River First Run Rum
1 ounce Lime Juice
½ ounce Maple Syrup
½ ounce Cointreau
2 dashes Allspice Dram
1½ ounces Black Tea, Chilled
Ice Ball
Lime Zest
Fresh Grated Nutmeg

Directions:
Shake the rum, lime juice, maple syrup, Cointreau, Allspice Dram, and black tea in a mixing tin.

Strain over a large ball of ice in a goblet. Garnish with lime zest and fresh grated nutmeg.

Mixed by Darren Crawford

TRANSCONTINENTAL

Ingredients:
1¼ ounces St. George Dry Rye Reposado Gin
¾ ounce Silo Solstice
¾ ounce Silo Cacao Vodka
3 dashes Nocino
Orange Peel

Directions:
Stir all ingredients in a mixing glass to dilution, then strain into a small cocktail glass.

Garnish with the oil of an orange peel.

Mixed by Darren Crawford

VERMONT RESOURCES

State Facts

Nickname: Green Mountain State
Mottos: Freedom and Unity, May the 14th Star Shine Bright

Flower: Red Clover
Tree: Sugar Maple
State Bird: Hermit Thrush

Borders: Massachusetts, New Hampshire, New York, and Canadian province of Quebec

Admission to Union: March 4, 1791
Population: 626,041 and Mimi Buttenheim (second least populated state)
Land Area: 9,620 sq mi (ranked 45th)
Counties: 14
Width: 80 miles
Length: 160 miles
Percent Water: 4.1
Population Density: 65.8/sq mi
Capital: Montpelier
Largest City: Burlington
Highest Point: Mt. Mansfield
Lowest Point: Lake Champlain
Latitude: 42 degrees 44' N to 45 degrees 1' N
Longitude: 71 degrees 28' W to 73 degrees 26' W

Brew Tours, Trails, and Driver Services

- In Okemo Valley, The Good Bus offers customizable brewery tours for groups of eight to twenty-four people.
- In Addison County, the Middlebury Tasting Trail offers a tour of some of Vermont's finest breweries.
- In the Mad River Valley, Vermont Bed & Brew offers discount lodging and a full day of craft beer touring without the worries of driving.

- Burlington Brew Tours offers preselected tours or guests can craft a private tour, while Burlington-based My Daddy's Caddy offers a stylish ride for smaller groups.
- Vermont Backroad Tours, based out of Wallingford, Vermont, has trips for ten to thirty beer lovers.
- In Stowe, jump on Umiak's Craft Brewery Tour. Visit seven breweries in the region on this guided brew tour. Leave the driving to your guide and enjoy a scenic brewery-to-brewery experience. (Source: VermontVacation.com)

Outdoor Activities

- Biking
- Boating
- Camping
- Canoeing
- Climbing
- Cross-Country Skiing
- Dog Sledding
- Downhill Skiing
- Fishing
- Golfing
- Hiking
- Horseback Riding
- Hunting
- Ice Hockey
- Ice Skating
- Kayaking
- Sailing
- Scuba Diving
- Snowboarding
- Snowmobiling
- Snowshoeing
- Swimming
- Tennis

Products Made in Vermont

- Beer and Wine
- Cider
- Dairy
- Fruits and Vegetables
- Honey
- Livestock and Poultry
- Maple
- Specialty Foods
- Stone
- Wood
- Wool and Fiber

Vermont products are made by craftspeople who take pride in their work. Breweries, wineries, cideries, and distilleries have proven an overwhelming success in such a small state. Their focus toward sustainability, local resources, innovative ideas, and patience through trying weather is why Vermont products are so cherished and in such high demand worldwide.

APPENDIX

Much of the research for this book was done through phone and in-person interviews with owners and staff. When that was not possible online resources were employed.

Resources

General Information about Vermont
  vermontvacation.com
  vermont.gov
  vermont.com
  vermont.org

Wineries

Vermont Grape and Wine Council
www.vermontgrapeandwinecouncil.com
http://en.wikipedia.org/wiki/Ice_cider

Wineries—Introduction by Sara & Chris Granstrom
  Artesano Meadery
  www.artesanomead.com

  Boyden Valley Winery & Spirits
  www.boydenvalley.com

  Brook Farm Vineyards
  www.brookfarmvineyards.com

  Champlain Orchards
  www.champlainorchards.com

  Charlotte Village Winery
  www.charlottevillagewinery.com

  East Shore Vineyard
  www.eastshorevineyard.com

  Eden Ice Cider Company & Winery
  www.edenciders.com

Fresh Tracks Farm Vineyard & Winery
www.freshtracksfarm.com

Hall Home Place Ice Cider
www. hallhomeplace.com

Huntington River Vineyard
www.huntingtonrivervineyard.com

Lincoln Peak Vineyards
www.lincolnpeakvineyard.com

Mad River Vineyard
www.madrivervineyard.com/the_grapes/default.html

Montcalm Vineyards
www.montcalmvineyards.com
www.vermontgrapeandwinecouncil.com/our-members/montcalmvineyards

Neshobe River Winery
www.neshoberiverwinery.com/index.php
www.brandon.org/things-to-do
www.neshoberiverwinery.com

Newhall Farm
www.newhallfarmvt.com/pages/about

North Branch Vineyards
www.northbranchvineyards.com

Otter Valley Winery
www.ottervalleywinery.com

Putney Mountain Winery
www.putneywine.com

Shelburne Vineyard
www.shelburnevineyard.com
www.winemakermag.com/924-sur-lie-wine-kits
www.winespectator.com/drvinny/show/id/52755

www.bloomberg.com/news/articles/2015-10-01/
what-is-p-t-nat-wine-an-ancient-winemaking-style-on-the-rise

Snow Farm Vineyard
www.snowfarm.com

Sugarbush Vineyard
www.hillisfarm.com

Whaleback Vineyard
www.whalebackvineyard.com

Distilleries

Vermont Distillers Association & Vermont Chapter of the USBG

Distilleries—Introduction by Mimi Buttenheim
Appalachian Gap Distillery
www.appalachiangap.com

Boyden Valley Winery & Spirits
www.boydenvalley.com

Caledonia Spirits
www.caledoniaspirits.com

Dunc's Mill
www.craftdistillerytours.com

Flag Hill Farm
www.flaghillfarm.com

Green Mountain Distillers
www.probrewer.com/library/used-tanks/tank-types
www.greendistillers.com

Mad River Distillers
www.madriverdistillers.com

Saxtons River Distillery
www.saxtonsriverdistillery.com

Shelburne Orchards Distillery
www.shelburneorchards.com/distillery

Silo Distillery
www.beerandbrewing.com/vermont-gets-its-own-maltster
www.brewing-distilling.com/page2/ccarl-stills.html
www.silodistillery.com

Smugglers' Notch
www.smuggs.com
www.smugglersnotchdistillery.com/spirits.php

Stonecutter Spirits
www.stonecutterspirits.com
www.coolhunting.com/food-drink/stonecutter-craft-spirits-vermont-
    barrel-aged-gin-whiskey
www.escapebrooklyn.com/middlebury-vt

Vermont Distillers
www.vermontdistillers.com
www.distilledvermont.org

Vermont Spirits Co.
www.vermontspirits.com

WhistlePig Whiskey
www.whistlepigwhiskey.com

Cideries

Cideries—Introduction by Colin Davis
    Citizen Cider
    www.citizencider.com
    www.pbs.org/thebotanyofdesire

    Eden Ice Cider Company
    www.edenciders.com

    Shacksbury
    www.shacksbury.com/home

    Stowe Cider
    www.stowecider.com

Woodchuck Cider
www.woodchuck.com/age-gate

Breweries

Vermont Brewers' Association www.vermontbrewers.com
American Brewers Guild Brewing School www.abgbrew.com
Vermont Pub and Brewery-Shannon Smith of www. AssociatedContent.com
www.vermontbrewers.com/wp-content/uploads/2015/03/Economic-
Impact- Vermont-Brewers-Association-112415.pdf
www.vermontbrewers.com/passport-program

Breweries—Introduction by Sean Lawson
1st Republic Brewing Co.
www.1strepublicbrewingco.com

14th Star Brewing
www.14thstarbrewing.com

Backacre Beermakers
www.backacrebeermakers.com/verify.php?return=/&x=-1
www.vermontbrewers.com/backacrebeer

Bent Hill Brewery
www.benthillbrewery.com/wphome

Bob Cat Café and Brewery
www.thebobcatcafe.com

Brewster River Pub and Brewery
www.brewsterriverpubnbrewery.com

Brocklebank Craft Brewing
www.brocklebankvt.com

Burlington Beer Co.
www.burlingtonbeercompany.com

Drop-In Brewing Co.
www.dropinbrewing.com

Farnham Ale & Lager
www.ratebeer.com/brewers/farnham-ale-lager-vt/25064

Fiddlehead Brewing Co.
www.fiddleheadbrewing.com

Foam Brewers
www.foambrewers.com
www.beeradvocate.com/beer/profile/45496

Foley Brothers Brewing
www.vermontbrewers.com/foleybrothers

Four Quarters Brewing
www.fourquartersbrewing.com

Frost Beer Works
www.frostbeerworks.com

Good Measure Brewing Co.
www.goodmeasurebrewing.com/home

Goodwater Brewery
www.goodwaterbreweryvt.com

Harpoon Brewery
www.harpoonbrewery.com

Hermit Thrush Brewery
www.hermitthrushbrewery.com

Hill Farmstead Brewery
hillfarmstead.com

Hop'n Moose Brewing Co.
www.vermontbrewers.com/hopnmoose
hopnmoose.wixsite.com/hopnmoose

House of Fermentology
www.houseoffermentology.com

Idletyme Brewing Co.
idletymebrewing.com

J'ville Brewery
www.jvillebrewery.com

Kingdom Brewing
www.vermontbrewers.com/kingdombrewing
www.kingdombrewingvt.com

Lawson's Finest Liquids
www.lawsonsfinest.com

Long Trail Brewing Co.
www.longtrail.com/age-verification?destination=node/2

Lost Nation Brewing
www.lostnationbrewing.com

Madison Brewing Co.
www.madisonbrewingco.com

Magic Hat Brewing Co.
www.magichat.net

McNeill's Pub and Brewery
www.vermontbrewers.com/mcneills

Northshire Brewery
www.northshirebrewery.com

Norwich Inn
www.norwichinn.com

Otter Creek Brewing
www.ottercreekbrewing.com/age-verification?destination=node/2

Prohibition Pig
www.prohibitionpig.com

Queen City Brewery
www.queencitybrewery.com

Red Barn Brewing
www.redbarnbrewingvt.com

River Roost Brewery
www.riverroostbrewery.com

Rock Art Brewery
www.rockartbrewery.com

Saint J Brewery
www.saintjbrewery.com

Simple Roots Brewing
www.simplerootsbrewing.com

Stone Corral Brewery
www.stonecorral.com

Switchback Brewing
www.switchbackvt.com

Ten Bends Beer
www.tenbendsbeer.com

The Alchemist
en.wikipedia.org/wiki/
Beer_rating#BeerAdvocate

Trout River Brewing Co.
www.troutriverbrewing.com

Vermont Pub & Brewery
www.vermontbrewery.com

von Trapp Brewing
www.onlyinyourstate.com/
vermont/heaven-earth-vt
www.vontrappbrewing.com

Whetstone Station Brewery
www.whetstonestation.com

Zero Gravity Craft Brewery
www.zerogravitybeer.com

Smugglers' Notch

Smugglers' Notch in Lamoille County, Vermont, separates Mount Mansfield, Vermont's highest peak, from Spruce Peak and the Sterling Range.

"Smugglers' Notch derives its name from activities precipitated by a request of President Thomas Jefferson to prevent American involvement in the Napoleonic Wars. The Embargo Act of 1807 forbade American trade with Great Britain and Canada. But proximity to Montreal made it a convenient trading partner, and the Act caused great hardship for Vermonters, many of whom continued the illegal trade with Canada, carrying goods and herding livestock through the Notch. Fugitive slaves also used the Notch as an escape route to Canada. The route was improved to accommodate automobile traffic in 1922, thus providing a route for liquor to be brought in from Canada during the Prohibition years." *source, Wikipedia*

Acknowledgments

Special thanks to Mimi Buttenheim, Alastair Windeler, Karl Uberbacher, and Heidi Melbostad for supporting this project, showing me the wonders of Vermont, driving through rain and snow and sleet and sunshine to distilleries, wineries, breweries, and cideries, and smiling most of the way through.

Thank you to the gracious people of Vermont, and to the support of the United States Bartenders' Guild Vermont Chapter.

Many thanks to the helpful staff and crew at Mad River Distillers for seasons of fun and inspiring this project.

And thanks to Sam von Trapp and his incredible staff for their support and his thoughtful foreword.

Many thanks to the expertise of Andie Ferman and Darren Crawford, who created cocktail recipes focused on Vermont flavors and products and prepared them for the drink photography in this book.

Thank you to my wonderful research assistants, Scott Mansfield and Megan Crowley.

Thank you to Skyhorse Publishing, and to Abigail Gehring for loving the Green Mountain State.

About the Author

Liza Gershman is an award-winning photographer and writer, as well as a seasoned world traveler. Passionate about food, people, and culture, she has had the opportunity to photograph in more than forty-three countries and forty-six US states during her career.

Liza teaches workshops, writes monthly articles on photography, and is a national speaker for Canon USA. She worked as the senior digital photographer for Williams-Sonoma, freelanced for Restoration Hardware, is a Getty Image contributor, and has photographed twelve cocktail and cookbooks.

Mixologists

Darren Crawford is a Bay Area, California native. Darren has more than two decades of experience in the food and beverage industry. Previously the bar manager at Bourbon & Branch in San Francisco, he most currently created and managed the bar program at The Devil's Acre in North Beach, California. Darren continues to execute amazing classics and pushes the boundaries with creative cocktail originals.

Andie Ferman is brand ambassador, director of education and hospitality, tasting room manager, boozer, and a shaker at St. George Spirits in Alameda, California. Since joining the team at St. George Spirits in April of 2006, Andie has witnessed and had the joy of taking part in the amazing growth of the industry through seminars and education, event management, and industry outreach. Andie thoroughly enjoys the art of liquid poetry, a chance to paint many colors and flavors on the canvas that is distilled spirit.

Cheers!